ENDORSEME

A mentor told me years ago to n̶ ̶ ̶̶̶̶̶̶ ̶s̶p̶e̶a̶k̶ beyond my own experiences. I have not known the depths of this kind of pain and grief
in my own life but have watched others walk through it. Jeff and
Stephen write from a perspective of walking through their personal losses and struggles. *Green Hearts* is the kind of book I want
to share with those around me who are walking their own difficult journeys.

> —**Denise Jones,** Christian music artist, Point of Grace
> Brentwood, TN

For forty plus years I have practiced medicine/surgery. During
that time I have seen hundreds and thousands of people experience tragedy, grief, and sorrow. Jeff and Stephen have now given
us a resource that reminds us that God is always in control and
He loves us in all circumstances. Their collection of stories (testimonies) is a powerful witness that God is all-powerful, all-
good, and all-knowing. True healing, whether physical or spiritual, is a continual process. There will always be a scar. *Green
Hearts* reminds me that Jesus indeed calmed the Sea of Galilee,
and there is no storm in our hearts that He cannot calm or heal.

> —**Randy W. Cooper, MD,** chief of surgery, University Hospital
> Augusta, GA
>
> Chairman of deacons, First Baptist Church
> North Augusta, SC

This book is rare. It never suggests Christians can sidestep life's
toughest issues. But there's warmth, hope, insight, and reassur-
ance of God's love and support through the darkest times. Every

chapter moved me and helped me. *Green Hearts* is a book for those who face struggles, which is all of us.

—**Dr. Alistair Brown**, Oxford, England, retired president of
Northern Seminary
Lisle, IL

In writing *Green Hearts*, Jeff Bumgardner and Dr. Stephen Cutchins have rendered a great service to the body of Christ. In my more than half-century of ministry, one of the most persistent questions I have been asked is, "Why do terrible things happen to Christians, and what do you do when it happens to you?"

Green Hearts answers these questions in inspiring, yet easy to understand ways. Putting a human face on the problem of grief by using the testimonies of real people who have experienced terrible tragedy gives *Green Hearts* even greater impact. I am ordering a steady supply of *Green Hearts* to share with people who are dealing with grief.

—**Dr. Richard Land**, president, Southern Evangelical Seminary
Charlotte, NC

Dr. Cutchins and Jeff Bumgardner have provided a book that contains some of the best of truths about some of the worst of times. Those who do not read it will miss experiencing the utmost about His highest in their lowest moments of life.

—**Dr. Norman Geisler**, Distinguished Senior Professor of
Theology and Apologetics, Southern Evangelical Seminary
Charlotte, NC

I am honored to commend and encourage this book to all who read it. The authors are men of God whose faith and character have been hammered out upon the anvil of heartbreak and hardship. They write not as theorists, but practitioners. They do not provide philosophies of suffering, but the reality of it. Suffering and death exert life-altering impact on all of us—our faith, our relationships, our future. You may not *want* to read this book, but you cannot avoid the need for its message and ministry to help provide a hope and a future beyond your present suffering. I recommend you read it.

> —**Dr. David H. McKinley,** pastor-teacher, Warren Baptist Church Augusta, GA

Green Hearts describes grief and loss with stunning clarity. If you have experienced grief, you will see yourself in the thoughts and actions, fears and pain, and feel to the depths of your soul the reality of loss on this messy planet. But you will also experience the hope of these who have walked in the darkest of days and can still say, "Though he slay me, yet will I trust in Him" (Job 13:15). That is the hope we have in Christ—"God did this so that . . . we who have fled to take hold of the hope set before us may be greatly encouraged. We have this hope as an anchor for the soul, firm and secure." (Hebrews 6:18-19b NIV)

> —**Dr. Norma Hedin,** provost, Dallas Baptist University Dallas, TX

What do you do when you are in the presence of God and worship will not come? As you read this compelling book, you will discover the stories of many who have been in that exact spot. There is tremendous help in the pages that are in front of you. As you consider the reality you face, you will also encounter a God who is big enough to redeem any situation!

> —**Dr. David B. Horton,** president, Fruitland Baptist Bible College, Hendersonville, NC

Have you ever noticed how a broken arm is easier to heal than a broken heart, a shattered dream, or a splintered life? In *Green Hearts*, Dr. Stephen Cutchins and Jeff Bumgardner offer help and hope for those whose emotional pain and grief is real and raw. They share from the depths of their own experiences of personal, painful loss, and they give a voice to others who share their own stories of hurt and recovery as well. The spot-on scriptural insights, combined with the testimonies, remind us that God is always incredibly good, even if life is sometimes terribly bad. There's healing here. I recommend this book.

> —**Dr. J. Kie Bowman,** senior pastor, Hyde Park Baptist /
> The Quarries Church
> Austin, TX

The longer I serve in ministry, the more I'm convinced that most of us don't know how to deal with pain. Stephen Cutchins and Jeff Bumgardner reminded me of my own times of heartbreak; but they also reminded me that God is infinitely good, even in the darkest moments of life. The stories in this book will break your heart, but they will also point to the comfort that broken hearts long for.

> —**Ryan Rush,** senior pastor, Kingsland Baptist Church
> Katy, TX

Whether asking *why* or *how* questions in the darkness of grief, *Green Hearts* shares light and hope. The reader will experience authentic empathy and help from fellow strugglers who have experienced the goodness of God in their darkest hours.

> —**Dr. Steve Cloud,** president, Vision Ventures
> Columbia, SC

Bumgardner and Cutchins share with every reader how to get help from God and His people to handle the emotional journey we all take sooner or later—the journey through grief. I was moved, blessed, and helped practically, and you will be too.

> —**Dr. Dick Lincoln,** retired pastor, Shandon Baptist Church
> Columbia, SC

Everyone has experienced, or will experience, grief and pain as we go through life. This collection of testimonies, words of explanation and counsel, and appropriate Bible passages should help every reader. Hearts that are "green" with bitterness and disappointment can become "green" with new vitality by reading this book.

> —**Dr. Thomas L. Constable,** senior professor emeritus of Bible exposition, Dallas Theological Seminary
> Dallas, TX

Grief is both universal and unique. We all face it, but the circumstances surrounding each loss and the relationships involved make it something hard to pin down when trying to comfort those in need of comforting. What I love about this book is that it doesn't try to give one definitive answer for the grieving, but it shows that loss and grief do not have to define you and that there will be a tomorrow when the sun will actually shine again. For those of us who have walked through these dark valleys, *Green Hearts* is a comforting recollection of where we've been. And for those who have yet to journey to that unfortunate place, it is a refreshing map to show the way across and through.

> —**Joel Lindsey,** Christian music songwriter and publisher
> Santa Barbara, CA

I was president at Southwestern Baptist Theological Seminary when several of our students were killed in the Wedgwood Baptist Church shootings. During the community-wide service honoring the lives of the students, one of the clergy prayed a simple prayer: "Father, thank You that You waste nothing. Amen." With honesty and transparency, Jeff Bumgardner and Stephen Cutchins share personal stories of grief and give comfort by reminding us that "God never wastes a hurt." He is still good in the worst of times. *Green Hearts* is help for those who are hurting.

> —**Ken Hemphill,** special assistant to the president for denominational relations, North Greenville University
> Tigerville, SC

GREEN HEARTS

God's Goodness in the Worst of Times

JEFF BUMGARDNER
DR. STEPHEN CUTCHINS

FOREWORD BY
DR. NORMAN GEISLER

Auxano
PRESS

ISBN: 978-0-615-19790-6

Published by Auxano Press, Travelers Rest, South Carolina, www.auxanopress.com.

Editorial and Project Management: Maleah Bell

Interior Design: CrosslinCreative.net

Cover design: 99designs

Cover image: Dino Buljubasic

Printed in the United States of America

23 22 21 20 19—5 4 3 2 1

This book is dedicated to our wives. It has been said, in ministry, a spouse can either double your impact or cut it in half. Our wives have consistently made us better men and increased our ministry impact over the years. Without their support and encouragement this book would be nothing more than an idea we discussed over a sushi lunch.

Thank you, Jody Bumgardner and
Wendy Cutchins!

CONTENTS

ACKNOWLEDGMENTS

First, we want to thank the people of First Baptist Church of North Augusta, South Carolina for their support. Our church is a church that prays! Thank you for loving us as we serve you joyfully week by week.

We would also like to thank Dr. Ken Hemphill for his vision for publishing works such as this one with the goal of helping churches grow.

In addition, we wish to thank the following people:

Our Families
Jody, Caleb, Abby, Ella, and Ava Bumgardner
Wendy, Madelyn, and Sarah Cutchins

Green Heart Stories
Dr. Alistair Brown
Dr. Fred Cutchins
Dr. Norman Geisler
Paige McLemore
Joshua Plaisance
Jeff Risk
Stephanie Vargas
Pastor James Wilson

FOREWORD

Dr. Norman Geisler

Life is not skipping from mountain peak to mountain peak. There are valleys. And the deepest valley I have been through was the loss of a daughter. I was speaking in the Asheville, North Carolina area when I got a call from my youngest daughter asking me to come home as soon as I could. I asked what had happened, and she told me that her older sister had committed suicide. There is nothing I have experienced in life like the loss of a child in that way. I drove home to Charlotte immediately. Looking back, I don't know how I ever got home through all the tears.

Recalling times of tragedy, when personal or close at hand, is not difficult. At such times, answers about God and evil seem elusive or unsatisfying. At some time or another, everyone wonders about the existence of evil and suffering in the world. Its presence has touched all, ravaged many, and perplexed thinking men throughout the ages.

Since evil seems to be real, then perhaps God is not. We experience the reality of evil, but we do not seem to experience the reality of God. Therefore, many atheists have argued that the existence of evil in the world proves there is no God. If God does exist, must we believe that God is cruel, compassionless, impotent, or nonexistent in order to deal with the reality of evil in the world?

This question is more than an abstract, philosophical one. It touches each and every one of us where we live. Man was created in the image of God and was placed on earth with the power of free choice, and through his willful free choice, brought evil into the world. Our moral nature is a testimony to the reality of a moral structure within the universe, and our cruelty is a testimony to the sinful nature within man. It also explains the basic frustration, loneliness, and alienation felt by man, who is cut off from a higher reality since he is no longer in a normal state.

We are right to ask about the existence of God, and we are right to ask the moral question. The Christian position provides answers to these questions because we do live in a world created by a moral, loving, and powerful God. This, in fact, is the optimism of Christianity. Since there is an all-powerful God who can defeat evil without destroying free choice, and since there is an all-loving God who wants to defeat evil without destroying free choice, then there is the assured hope that He will defeat evil in the future.

The ultimate optimism of Christianity is that in the future there will be a time when evil is rendered null and void. But Christianity holds more than just the ultimate hope of the eventual defeat of evil. It provides immediate satisfaction and power to deal with the sinful nature of man. God desires to restore man to a vital personal relationship with Himself through man's faith in God, through the death of Jesus Christ for man's sin. The debt of sin and evil has been paid, and man has only to receive it.

Life is not skipping from mountain peak to mountain peak. There are valleys, and God can see you through the deepest valley. The suicide of your child is one of the worst possible things that can happen to you. You can't imagine how bad it is. But God's grace is sufficient. He is there when you go through the valley of the shadow of death, and He was with my family. He gave us the strength to go through it. After over sixty years of marriage, my wife and I have come to realize that God is supremely good when He gives and no less good when He denies. Even crosses from His gracious hand are blessings in disguise.

CHAPTER 1

WELCOME

his book is a mess. The power of this simple statement will become more apparent to you as you read the stories of tragedy, pain, and loss that make up its heart. What you are about to read is a collection of messy stories that highlight God's goodness in the worst of times. We all know what it means to be captured by the difficulty of life. If we are honest, there are days when our circumstances consume us with tough questions. Many times these questions go unanswered or, at best, inadequately answered. We make no guarantees of answering every question about why bad things happen in our lives. But we all have a story.

We hope that you will be encouraged as we expose the goodness of God revealed in the worst of times. Everyone experiences pain. It is the common ground on which all humanity stands. This book presents some of the most tragic and painful situations of life and answers the hard question of *why* from a Christian perspective. The why behind this collection of stories connects with the title *Green Hearts*. The inspiration for this book comes from the sudden death of Jeff's ten-year-old daughter, Ella, who loved hearts and the color green.

Our Inspiration | October 5, 2016

Ella was only ten years old when she found herself lying on the cold, hard tile of her church welcome center. Tears dripped from her chin as she cried out to her two sisters that she had lost her vision. What began with an abrupt pain in her head was quickly becoming debilitating. Without warning, an arteriovenous malformation (AVM) had ruptured in her brain. The bleed was massive and began shutting down her faculties within minutes. First, her eyesight. Then her speech. Soon Ella's ability to move her head and control her extremities had been lost. She was dying, and there was nothing anyone could do to save her.

When paramedics arrived, they struggled to understand what had occurred. Through facial expressions, Ella showed her disapproval to smelling salts as they strapped her to a stretcher and rushed her through the glass doors of the church toward the ambulance. However, this would only become known as her final response to outward stimulations. Before she could reach the hospital, she lost her ability to breathe on her own, as the catastrophic bleed spread further throughout her brain.

Upon Ella's arrival the hospital staff began to intubate her, as they wrestled to understand what was happening inside this sweet, innocent little girl. The CAT scan soon revealed the AVM that was located near her brainstem, as one family's routine, church activity-filled Wednesday soon became a nightmare.

This story is one of tragedy, loss, and devastation. It is a story of heartache and mourning. Ella's untimely death destroyed the innocence of childhood for her brother and sisters and shook the very foundation of faith that her parents spent their entire married life building and modeling for their family. Where is God's love in the sudden death of a seemingly healthy child? Where is God's mercy in the midst of an unimaginable tragedy? Where is God's goodness when a family devoted to serving Him is forced to let go of their baby girl?

After struggling to answer these difficult questions in real life and in real time, we felt the responsibility and inspiration to commit to paper the book that you now read. Though hundreds of people were praying for Ella, her story does not end with miraculous healing. Instead, it is a story that is still being written through the lives of those she left behind. Her story is personal to her family, but many other families have stories of their own. Tragedy comes when we least expect it, and it changes the core of who we are. Ella's story is the basis for this book, but this book is not Ella's story. Instead, it is your story and the story of anyone who has experienced the devastating effect of tragedy.

How We See It

As coauthors we are committed to talking directly to you, the reader, from three viewpoints. First, we want you to hear us from a personal perspective. Imagine the two of us sitting in your living room or meeting you for coffee or lunch at your favorite spot. As we write we have in mind various conversations we've had through the years with neighbors, friends, and family. Some of the most powerful lessons are learned outside of the classroom through casual gatherings with those we trust most. We want to connect with you through this book, the way we would around the dinner table after a great meal.

Many times our thoughts are jumbled in our minds and only come untangled as they are committed to a conversation or the pages of a journal. Our unique connection through the words on these pages is designed to generate new thoughts about God's goodness in the worst of times. Each new tragedy we experience creates a new weight and a new normal of pain management in our lives. We hope that the stories we share in this book will connect or reconnect you with the goodness of God.

Second, we are also pastors. As we write to you, we pull from thousands of conversations with people all over the country who have given us the privilege to serve them as spiritual leaders along their journey. Having collectively served eleven congregations in seven different states, spreading from California to the Carolinas, it is clear that all people value having a trusted ear to hear their stories of pain. Our calling to ministry regularly puts us in place to be that ear for others.

These interactions frequently happen in lobbies and hallways before or after events and services. They also occur behind the closed doors of our private offices when people are in the darkest moments of their lives. Because both of us have walked through tragedies, we have ourselves been the beneficiaries of pastoral care from trusted spiritual leaders. These leaders have been there when we found ourselves stuck in grief, pain, and the mixture of emotions that ooze out when we experience the worst of times. The benefit of pastoral care and counseling is a gift from God. We value the pastors in our lives and consider it a joy to serve others in that ancient relationship of care and protection.

Third, we write to you not only from personal and pastoral viewpoints but also from a practical viewpoint. God never wastes a hurt. Seeing His goodness in the worst of times is not just a passive thought process. God redeems the worst moments of our lives by calling us to *take action.*

One way to respond to pain is to become overwhelmed to the point that we *reject* the reality of the situation. We can get stuck in denial and attempt to continue moving forward as if nothing happened. But it did happen. A second option is to *receive* the weight of the pain to the point that we find it impossible to move forward because we believe that nothing good can ever happen again. But good things will happen. A third option that we would like you to consider is allowing God to *redeem* the situation.

> God works in our lives by redeeming the worst parts of us, and He never wastes a hurt.

God works in our lives by redeeming the worst parts of us, and He never wastes a hurt. As you experience each story collected in *Green Hearts*, don't hesitate to take practical action steps to move forward into the goodness of God for your life. We want you to be encouraged to the point that it overflows into action. Use the stories, biblical examples, and timeless truths presented in this book as nourishment and fuel as you discover God's goodness in the worst of times.

Introductions

Thank you for going on this journey with us. All the stories you read in this book are real. Some are transcribed from face-to-face interviews and will feel more conversational. Each chapter features at least one story. Throughout *Green Hearts*, we also take the opportunity to speak directly to you in sections titled "Author's Comments." As we begin our journey, let us introduce you briefly to Ella and other individuals who have graciously allowed us to share their stories with you.

Dr. Alistair Brown: Alistair is an innovative leader who has served as a pastor, professor, and seminary president. Since his retirement he continues to speak and lecture. His story is in chapter 3.

Ella Bumgardner: Ella is the inspiration for *Green Hearts*. In her ten years of life, she made a huge impact that continues to inspire. Her story is woven throughout this book. By reading it, you become a part of her legacy.

Dr. Fred Cutchins: Fred was an educator, counselor, and father of coauthor Stephen Cutchins. His passion was helping people deal with the stresses of life. Fred was a serious student of God's Word and served as both a deacon and teacher in his church. His story is in chapter 2.

Dr. Norman Geisler: For many years Dr. Norman Geisler has been an author, speaker, and seminary professor. We cannot adequately describe what a joy it is to have him write the foreword to this book. He has always taken the time to answer our tough questions, and we appreciate his support for this project. His story is in chapter 3.

Paige McLemore: Paige is a wife, mother, and public-school educator. She is also a Bible teacher in her church and regularly shares her journey as a guest speaker. Her story is in chapter 7.

Joshua Plaisance: Joshua is a kidney recipient from Ella Bumgardner. His story is in chapter 6.

Jeff Risk: Jeff is a businessman and entrepreneur with a passion for reaching people around the world with the gospel. He is also the president of a Christian nonprofit that focuses its efforts in China. His story is in chapter 5.

Stephanie Vargas: Stephanie is a heart and lung recipient from Ella Bumgardner. Stephanie's story is in chapter 6.

James Wilson: James is a children's pastor, husband, and father. He grew up experiencing numerous personal setbacks and physical challenges. Despite a difficult beginning he is a strong Christian influence for many. His story is in chapter 4.

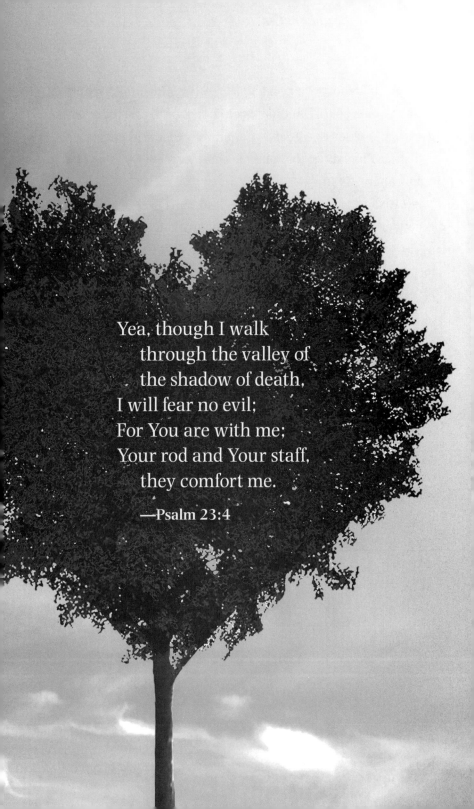

Yea, though I walk
   through the valley of
   the shadow of death,
I will fear no evil;
For You are with me;
Your rod and Your staff,
   they comfort me.

—Psalm 23:4

GRIEF

Life After Tragedy

G rief is natural, and it is awful. It claims your identity and turns you into someone you no longer recognize. Grief takes over your consciousness, filling it with questions and doubts. It invades your dreams with horrific panic and alternate realities. Tragedy is like a dark passenger that viciously reminds us there are things outside of our control. However, in the midst of tragedy, it is essential to understand that we have options. Although it seems as though control is completely taken out of our hands, options remain.

We can allow tragedy to defeat us or we can use it to find strength. Admittedly, finding strength is easier said than done. The natural thing to do is to give in to the pain and accept the misery of defeat and loss as a result. That feels right at the moment. It even makes sense when we allow our minds to follow the natural way of thinking. We tell ourselves we are honoring what we have lost. However, defeat is a lie that we must refuse to believe.

Author's Comments

JEFF In the months following Ella's death, I viewed grief as an enemy. Over time, I have come to embrace grief as a friend. While this idea may seem ridiculous, it is something with which I have become well acquainted. If I try to fight grief, I lose every time. When I embrace it, I learn to use it to propel me forward. Instead of battling against my natural tendencies to suppress thoughts and feelings in order to avoid emotion, I allow them to surface. Of course, these are private times. I try not to display my meltdowns for the general public to witness. But anger and denial are worse when they are pent up. I have found that when I deal with them quickly, I am ready to move on to the next moment. When I suppress them, they are still there in the moments ahead.

Death is the absence of life. Ella will forever be a huge part of who I am; so a huge part of who I am died on October 7, 2016. I will never be the same person I was before that day. The comfort I find is that I don't have to be that same person. I don't have to be the person who had not yet learned to live with tragedy. I don't have to be the dad who took for granted that his children would always be here. There is still life in me, and I will live that life to the fullest. If we face hardships and remain unchanged, we gain nothing from our losses. If we must dance with defeat, we need to choose to take the lead and let the spotlight shine as we find the beauty in the aftermath. There is a reason Earth is not called heaven. Tragedy is the very soil on which we walk in this life. While we may stumble over heartache and trial, healing and strength lay waiting to embrace us.

One moment we had Ella; the next she was gone. We never know what the next moment is going to hold for us. But we cannot walk through life in fear. Instead, we must choose to embrace the tragedy—finding our new identity within it—or live in defeat, refusing to honor our loss. I will never be the same as I was before losing Ella. Accepting this, I can choose to live my life in her honor by loving those around me.

Bitter or Better

What is the hardest thing you have been through lately? The hardest situations in life offer us the choice to become either bitter or better. One of the things that makes a positive difference in tough situations is talking through the issues. When Paul prayed for people in the Bible, he never asked God to change their circumstances. Instead, he asked God to make them better in their circumstances. Although it is hard to do, talking with God, family, and friends in difficult times can help you push back bitterness and become a better person. Tough times can throw you off-balance. God speaks primarily through His Word, so when you go through a tough situation, spend extra time in the Bible. Visualize a balancing scale, and put your thoughts about your situation on one side of the scale. On the other side of the scale, put the truth found in Scripture. As you talk with God, family, and friends, let the truth help you find balance.

Talking with God

One of the benefits of a relationship with God is that we have direct access to Him through prayer. However, prayer is sometimes misunderstood to be our way of getting God to change our circumstances. To enjoy the *power* of prayer, we must understand the *purpose* of prayer. God is not a genie in a bottle. He is an all-knowing, all-powerful, all-good Being who desires to pour out His blessings on His people. Prayer is not our way of getting our will done in heaven. Prayer is God's way of getting His will done on earth. When we pray, the question is not "God, can you hear me now?" The question is actually from God: "Can you hear Me now?"

> Prayer is not our way of getting our will done in heaven. Prayer is God's way of getting His will done on earth.

Hearing from God and being obedient to what He says is the power of prayer in our lives. When we ask for the things that line up with God's will, He hears us. When we talk with God, it is essential to understand that He is more concerned with our character development than our comfort. Share with God about your situation, and ask Him to give you the wisdom to see things from His perspective. "If any of you lacks wisdom, let him ask God, who gives generously to all without reproach, and it will be given him" (James 1:5 ESV).

Talking with Family

Although everyone in your family may not be trustworthy, open up to the ones who are, and share your struggles with them.

Your family is there to support you. We are often hesitant to open up about struggles because we don't want to come across as being weak. The problem is, we wind up walking alone in isolation even when surrounded by people who love us. Isolation is a breeding ground for bitterness. Sharing your weakness with trusted family members makes you stronger. "Two are better than one, because they have a good reward for their toil. For if they fall, one will lift up his fellow. But woe to him who is alone when he falls and has not another to lift him up!" (Ecclesiastes 4:9-10 ESV).

Talking with Friends

Trust is built in drops and lost in buckets. One of the most valuable resources a person can have is a trusted friend. Real friendships are built on trust, and trust is built with consistency over time. Are you spending enough time building trusted friendships? Who in your life has been consistent over time and has earned your trust? Social media trains us to think of friendship shallowly and distantly. Those types of friendships will not be of much help when the hard times come. Talking with a trustworthy friend in tough times makes you better instead of bitter. "A friend loves at all times, / and a brother is born for adversity" (Proverbs 17:17).

Author's Comments

STEPHEN

I remember the death of my dad a few weeks before I graduated from Winthrop University. He and his brother were the first in my family to graduate from college, and both went on to complete doctoral degrees. His father never finished high school, and it was a big deal for my dad to be in attendance the day I walked across the graduation stage to receive my college degree. I remember the conversations we had about how proud he would be that I had followed in his footsteps.

Although my dad died years ago, I still feel a sense of injustice from having watched him suffer for years with kidney failure and dialysis, only to die at a young age. His death brought me (as a 21-year-old) to a place of emptiness, confusion, and pain that I had not experienced before. I was overwhelmed by it. What made it worse was that I had no answer as to why things had turned out the way they did.

My dad and I had a special relationship, and he was the person I looked up to most in the world. When I was just a boy he would take me fishing regularly. I also remember him holding me in his arms and asking me if I knew how much he loved me. His answer was always, "Big much." In my heart and mind, I can still hear his voice saying those words today as if he were standing in the room with me. "Big much" was his way of keeping the message simple, clear, and memorable.

Despite his being diagnosed with kidney failure when I was in middle school, my dad continued to work full-time while on home dialysis well into my high school years. He also continued to be a loving, caring, and available father. I remember many late nights when he and I would hang around in the kitchen after my mom went to bed. We would eat leftovers and talk about whatever was on my mind. Reflecting on it, I realize now that his sickness was in many ways a gift to me because he was less consumed with work and more available.

Growing up with sickness in your immediate family changes the way you see each moment. Watching the man you most admire decline slowly and die during your developmental years changes the way you see the world. He eventually retired on disability, and I went off to college. There is much of his story that I missed over the next four years. However, one thing never changed. I would always call him when I couldn't get my head right.

The word that describes my dad best: *Wisdom*.

Fred Cutchins was a serious student of God's Word and served as both a deacon and teacher in his church. He was one of the wisest and best-studied men in my small hometown. He earned a PhD in counseling psychology from Georgia State University in 1976, the year before my birth. When I was born, my brother was sixteen, and my sister was twelve. I grew up as the "baby" of the family and also like an only child because my siblings were so much older than I.

My dad was a reserved and private man. Just weeks before he died, I was at home visiting. It was the first weekend in December, and I had come home from college to study and prepare for exams. I can remember spending time with him and enjoying conversations, yet again, with him about life. At this point, his health was not good, but he was at home. One moment from that weekend stands out from the rest. He asked me to help him get dressed.

Neither of us knew that would be one of our last times together. There was a moment when we looked at each other, and it felt as if our hearts and minds connected deeply. I knelt to help him put on his socks and shoes for the day and glanced up to see his eyes already looking in my direction. Neither of us said a word, but the connection between a son and his father has never been so strong. I could sense his gratitude and love toward me.

I returned to college, and he died only a few weeks later. I can still remember being woken up in the night. I received the phone call that I had dreaded since the day he was diagnosed with kidney failure years before: "Your father has died." His presence in my life up to that point had been constant and stabilizing. A new and unwelcomed normal began to take over my heart.

The days and years after my dad's death were not easy ones. There were so many ways our lives were intertwined that each day became a journey of absence. He would miss the birth of my children. They would never know him the way I did. Today, I tell my two daughters that he would have loved to know them. However, it is not the same as having him there asking them, "Do you know how much I love you?" I am sure his answer would be "Big much!"

At times the waves of grief would come and go. As the years went by, the pain seemed to be fading away, and I would begin to think that my journey with grief had ended. It became more natural and more comfortable to talk about him without tearing up and wrestling back the grief. I thought I was finally done with swallowing back the pain and could move on with only the happiness of the great memories I had made with my dad.

Years after I thought I had mastered the art of moving on from grief, I was driving across town to work one morning. I was in my first job as a public school teacher. It was a typical spring day; the sun was shining, and I was enjoying a cup of coffee in the car as I thought about the day ahead. I had gotten up early for a long run; I was training for a marathon. I felt on top of the world as I listened to my favorite playlist in the car on the way to work. My mind was free to think and dream, and I began to find myself deep in thought about something. Honestly, I don't remember what it was, and it doesn't matter. I got to the point that I couldn't seem to get my mind right about whatever it was. I was stuck.

Out of sheer habit, I grabbed my cell phone and called my dad. I was so deep into the routine of my day that I had forgotten he had died. The previous routine of calling my dad for all those years when I had a question and was stuck had resurfaced momentarily. I wasn't thinking; I even held the phone up to my ear and let it ring several times before it hit me. He is not there. He is not going to answer.

At that moment the grief of losing my dad flooded into that perfect morning and wrecked me all over again. I had to pull over to the side of the road, where I cried and cried for the better part of an hour. I even had to call in sick that morning. I think I cried more intensely in that moment than I had the weeks and months after his death.

Grief has a way of hanging around.

Denial

Grief is a strange thing, and denial is like a drug. Most of us are aware of the varying stages of grief. It taps you on the shoulder as you look at a picture, just to tease you into believing for a brief second that maybe it's all a dream. It haunts you in your sleep and awakens you to the realization of the pain all over again. It's ugly. It's merciless. It's every day. You are cognitive of what has happened, but denial has you living as if nothing has changed. It wraps you in a memory, allows you to smile, and then fades away as you feel a jab in the gut, as if you have been stabbed with a dull knife.

Yet, because denial gives you the gift of momentary escape from the pain, it keeps you wanting more—like an addiction. However, we can choose joy, even when denial pays an unexpected visit. We must be intentional about reaching beyond denial to accept the new normal. Embracing what can never be means letting go of what is.

> Embracing what can never be means letting go of what is.

Middle-School Bully

Like a middle school bully, grief intimidates us. It tells us we are worthless. It makes us feel defeated. Even when we try to find every way possible to avoid it, it finds us. We should approach grief the way we would deal with a bully. We take deep breaths, suppress the nerves, and attempt to face it head-on day after day.

Time is a major factor in our ability to reason with grief, but our hearts do not hurt any less today than they did the moment we first felt the pain. We simply learn how to look for joy and happiness through the tears. It's like a light in the darkness; we can choose to focus on the darkness or admire the glow of the light.

On those hard days, when you are looking for every way possible to find a different hall to walk down or a hidden path home, remember that grief is a bully from which you can't hide. So, call it out by name, look it in the eyes, and don't back down. When you finally face grief, you will find that the beauty of loss is not in what you no longer have but in the things that can never be taken from you.

Maybe you've never known grief in a personal way. Or maybe you and grief are on a first-name basis. Whatever the case, tragedy comes to visit when we least expect it; and more often than not, grief becomes a close companion as a result. So whether we find ourselves walking in grief or have yet to experience its presence, we are wise to recognize that it is a reality all of us will eventually face.

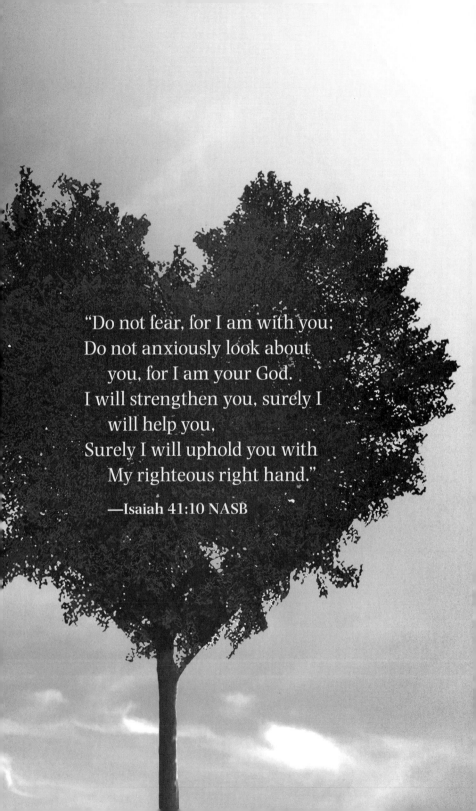

"Do not fear, for I am with you;
Do not anxiously look about
    you, for I am your God.
I will strengthen you, surely I
    will help you,
Surely I will uphold you with
    My righteous right hand."

—Isaiah 41:10 NASB

CHAPTER 3

GRIEVING

Suicide of a Daughter | Dr. Norman Geisler

We have six children: three boys and three girls. Our middle daughter was a problem child in our home and was very difficult for us. We prayed. We worked with her. We did everything we could.

One day, as I was speaking in the Asheville, North Carolina area, I received a phone call from my younger daughter. She said, "Come home as soon as you can."

I asked, "Why—what's happened?"

She answered, "I'll tell you when you get here."

I responded, "No, tell me now."

"My sister has committed suicide."

We've never experienced anything in life like the loss of a child. The loss of a child that way. I drove home immediately to Charlotte. I don't know how I got home through all the tears. Some of the family was already there, and we had to console them. We also had to make funeral arrangements; and while we were making the arrangements, our phone was ringing a lot.

The phone calls increased, and we were getting calls from people such as Ravi Zacharias and John Ankerberg and other well-known Christians from around the country. They all gave us words of encouragement, and they were all helpful. Almost everybody said "We are praying for you"; and, "Please know we are sorrowing with you," and so forth.

However, one caller, John Ankerberg, hit all the nails on the head. I don't know if he was formally trained or just naturally said it. Perhaps God gave him the words. In a two-minute phone call John said the four most encouraging things that could be said to somebody going through a situation such as ours. The fourth thing, you would never guess in a million years.

"I love you."

"I'm praying for you."

"I grieve with you."

"It's not your fault."

His last statement hit me like a ton of bricks. I thought, "What if I had done this or that? What if I had been a better father? What if I had been a better husband? What if I had spent more time with my daughter?" What if . . . what if . . ., and soon I was "what-iffing" myself to death. I said to myself, "Well, wait a minute"—we already have one person dead here. But they're going to have two people dead if I keep on this path."

I wasn't there. I wouldn't have done it. I wouldn't have encouraged her to do it. I would have stopped it if I could have; but I couldn't. It was out of my control. God's in control; I'm not. But the words "It's not your fault" just rang in my ears.

I was laying guilt on myself that was unnecessary. I had guilt that was untrue. I didn't kill the person. I don't encourage that. I don't encourage that to happen to anyone. But it happened, and God reached down and began to encourage me. I talked to another Christian who had lost his wife, and his words were encouraging too. "I love you; I'm praying for you; I'm sympathizing with you; it's not your fault" were the four statements that encouraged me.

I was president of Southern Evangelical Seminary at the time. Although students and faculty members were trying to encourage me, I was tired of answering all the questions. I got so tired of telling the story. However, I realized that every time I told it I healed a little bit more. Several weeks after my daughter died, I said, "I'm just going to give a whole message in chapel about this." I was told later that I was the only one not crying. By that time, I had no more tears left to cry. God had given me the greatest opportunity to provide this message to the entire student body.

> God is good when He gives supremely good; no less when He denies.

I heard later that Andy Stanley was using the recording for his grief counseling. Others were encouraged to know that God can see us through the deepest valley. When we go through the valley of the shadow of death, He's there; and He was with us.

My wife and I have come to realize that God is good when He gives supremely good; no less when He denies. Even crosses from His gracious hand are blessings in disguise. That summarizes what was happening in our lives. The worst thing that ever happened to us was the suicide of our daughter. You can't imagine how bad it was. But God's grace is sufficient. It really is. He gave us the strength to go through the hard time.

My wife and I have been married for sixty-one years now. We have fifteen grandchildren and six great-grandchildren. We've been able to invest in a lot of lives during our lifetime. God was gracious in giving us so many children and grand-children, even though this happened to us.

The temptation that comes to people when this happens is from the devil, and there *is* a devil. He is alive on planet Earth. The devil said to me, "Who are you to go around the country telling people how to live when you had a daughter who com-mitted suicide." He wants to shut our mouths, and he doesn't want us to say another word to anyone else. We have to resist the temptation to listen to him.

Who am I? Just a sinner saved by grace. I'm not perfect, and my children aren't perfect. But remember this: God is a perfect Father. He made perfect creatures called *angels*. He gave them a perfect home called heaven. One-third of them rebelled and never returned. Do I expect to do better than God?

Author's Comments

JEFF

As you read this, you may be thinking, "As a believer Dr. Geisler will see his daughter again one day." Yes, I agree. I also believe I will see Ella again in heaven. But some days heaven seems so far away. Some days I'm not OK with that. Sometimes I don't want anyone else to make that comment. Why? Because I'm not OK with not having Ella here.

For those of you who are where we are, or have been there at some point in your life, I know that you understand. As a believer I have the comfort of the Holy Spirit and God's grace to sustain me. As believers we don't grieve as the world grieves. But we still grieve. Grief is real. It is all-consuming and devastating.

Never try to tell someone how to grieve. Never try to make it better or OK, because it's not OK. It's just not. Simply love. Just love us and be there. You don't have to relate to me. You don't have to know what to say. Just be there.

Honor the Past by Not Living in It

The past is powerful. For many of us, there is a fear of moving forward in faith. When an organization or an individual begins to look and move forward, it may feel as though the past is not honored. However, the past has brought you to where you are and has prepared you to take the next step. The past prepares you for progress. Our past was not designed to get us where we are. Our past was designed by God to get us where we are going.

Moving forward in faith is uncomfortable because it requires change. But God is more concerned with our character development than our comfort level. He has plans for each of us, and His plans involve change. The only constant thing

> Our past was not designed to get us where we are. Our past was designed by God to get us where we are going.

25

in this world is change. What got you here will not keep you here. God is the Unchanging Changer of all things. He is the Unmoved Mover of all things. He loves you enough not to leave you alone. Are you honoring the past by not living in it?

Most of us tend to look at the past through the lens of whatever situation we are facing currently. If we are sharing a fun evening with friends, we will often recount a humorous story of something that happened to us or someone we know. If we are hesitant to chase a big dream because fear has paralyzed us, we are likely to look back at situations where we failed. We convince ourselves that this action justifies our inaction and that the pursuit of the dream is not worth the sacrifice because it will just end in disaster.

Similarly, in times when we are struggling emotionally with a loss or some hardship, we look back over the years through the lens of sadness and grief. In such cases, even happy times are discolored by our current emotion as we long to relive those happy moments. Perhaps we can even hear the soundtrack from a sad movie scene playing in our mind. Our emotions can take us from the height of the tallest mountain to the depths of the deepest valley. They are the centerpiece of what makes us human.

However, if we are not careful, we can allow our response to tragedy to be driven strictly by our emotions. Doing so can become dangerous over time as our decisions and behavior change with our mood, causing us to view ourselves as victims instead of victors. When emotion-driven responses take root in our lives, we create a false narrative, and the recovery process cannot begin.

How do we honor something that has caused us so much pain? When something is taken from us, whether it's a job, a relationship, a loved one, or a possession, a natural response is to do everything we can to avoid the subject. However, avoidance becomes suppression with the potential to cause higher levels of pain over a more significant amount of time. When our grief is great, it is because the gift was great. When we honor the loss, we honor the gift.

Author's Comments

STEPHEN

I want you to know that I go to counseling, and I am not ashamed. Getting the help of a counselor is nothing to be embarrassed about, despite what others might think. I grew up in a home with a father who had a PhD in counseling psychology. Because of this, I believed that I could never need a counselor. I was wrong. When I was in my early thirties, a mentor of mine mentioned in passing that he went to see a counselor. I was surprised. Why was he in counseling? He was a stable and successful leader who seemed to have it all together. I came to realize that one of the reasons he was so stable and successful was his commitment to receiving counseling.

Our family moved to Austin, Texas when I was in my late thirties. Having lived in the Carolinas all of our adult lives, our family was ready and excited about this new adventure. Shortly after we landed and got settled, my wife's father died. Because we were not yet connected with people in our new environment, we felt distant and isolated as the grieving process began to settle in on my wife. It affected all of us as she was hurting. It hurt because it mattered.

Most of our family and long-term friends were on the East Coast and we felt alone. During this challenging time we needed help. Wendy and I reached out to a married couple in Austin who were both professional counselors. We began meeting with them together, and they guided us through the grieving process. Wendy and I grew stronger together during this time with the help of this couple. We continue to meet with them and are healthier people as a result.

Don't just sit in your pain. Get help. Take action and get unstuck. Small hinges can swing big doors, and counseling can be a hinge to help you move out of your pain. As a pastor, I share openly with people about the fact I go to counseling, in order to normalize getting help. Life is hard; get help when you need it. We all need help from outside ourselves. You can't pick up a bathtub if you're sitting in it.

Depression | Dr. Alistair Brown

I was the pastor of a growing church. I was liked and appreciated, and our numbers kept going up. But my world had grown very dark deep inside my head and my heart. I couldn't see value in my work, couldn't believe people were being helped, couldn't see a future that was good. I might have said that God seemed a million miles away, but the truth was that I had no idea where God was at all. I still believed in Him, but somehow

I had become completely lost. "You're depressed," my doctor told me. And I was. Not just tired or sad or feeling down. Seriously depressed. But I was still working.

The following Sunday night we baptized ten people. Services like that were always big occasions because family and friends were invited and came. The place was packed. I stood up and preached a message I believed but didn't feel. Inside I was dead. I had no sense of God and no sense that the message mattered. I just wanted to get through the service.

The sermon finished, we sang a hymn; my associate and one of the elders baptized the people, and then it was back to me. Every baptism service was an evangelistic opportunity, so it was now my job to call people to commitment. I wished I could have done anything else at that moment. Only grim determination got me to the front of the church, and I invited people to give their lives to Christ, for the first time or in a deeper commitment. I said the right kind of words and stopped. What happened next was nothing I expected.

It was with deep darkness chilling my heart and with no sense at all of God's presence that I gave a call to faith. Then I stopped and waited. Nothing. No one moved. And then they did. To my utter amazement, two college students came to the front. My associate pastor nodded to counselors to join them. Then a family came. More counselors needed. Then a woman I had never seen before came all on her own. Then six or eight more students. A man and his wife. A child of about twelve. And more and more.

My associate ran out of counselors. Still more walked to the front—some in tears, some with faces shining. In the past we had seen six, seven, or even ten people respond at a service; but that night about thirty came. My mind could not have been in more pain. My heart could not have been duller. My faith could not have been less. But amazingly, crazily, in that service we had the largest response our church had ever seen.

I learned two things that night. First, I learned that God is never far away, no matter what we feel. His presence—and His power—do not depend on our feelings and not even on our faith. That night I was dead on the inside and the least expectant evangelist in the land, but God changed many eternal destinies before my eyes. Even when God seems lost to us, He is always there and always at work.

Second, I learned that not even a wonderful spiritual moment is a quick fix for depression. I left that service as soon as I could, got in my car, and drove to the top of a hill overlooking the city. As I stared out at the lights and the dark sky, I cried and cried in deep misery. I had seen God do remarkable things just an hour before; but still I felt lost and that my work was for nothing. Depression is not ended easily.

One Sunday, near the end of the service, I explained to the congregation that I had depression and would be gone for a couple of weeks to rest and recover. Afterward, many came to me, assured me of their prayers, and said words of encouragement. There was a remarkable number who whispered, "I've been depressed for years. Thank you for being honest. What medication are you on?" We had quite an exchange of "You're taking that; oh, I take this."

Not one person out of hundreds who came to the church condemned me. I was met only with love, understanding, and patience. Many told me of their depression, but until that moment they'd kept it secret. Christians all too often keep depression a secret, and some speak of it as a failure of faith. This deeply distresses me. I have spoken about depression at conferences of pastors, and almost nothing else I have ever said has drawn such a positive response. Many have told me of their struggles, but mostly their congregations knew nothing of their pain.

By the way, I was not off work for two weeks. It was five months, and I went back only then because of difficult situations among the church leaders (not related to my illness). It took two and a half years for me to come out of my darkness. But I did come out, and I have never gone back there. There is healing, good life, and good ministry after depression.

> How long, LORD? Will you forget me forever?
>> How long will you hide your face from me . . .
> But I trust in your unfailing love;
>> my heart rejoices in your salvation.
> I will sing the LORD's praise,
>> for he has been good to me. (Psalm 13:1, 5-6 NIV)

For David, the psalmist, the day came when his depression ended, and he lived again in the joy of God's presence. And, for Alistair Brown, the day came when my depression ended. The joy of living in God's presence has been mine, too, and I have never returned to the hopelessness of those times. No matter how long the night of darkness lasts, there are always good days ahead with God. May our loving Lord be with you, whether or not you sense his presence right now.

In his hand is the life of
every living thing
and the breath of all
mankind.

—Job 12:10 ESV

CHAPTER 4

QUESTIONS

Why?

Every one of us can think of a time when we cried out to God, "Why me?" Everyone experiences pain; that fact is the common ground on which all humanity stands. Every living person is in the process of pain management. The *real* question is *why* must it be this way? Why must we deal with pain and suffering? Why doesn't God help us? Why doesn't He heal the sick? Why doesn't He stop women from being raped? Why must people we love die?

These issues are real life issues of the heart. However, the question of *why* must be resolved in the mind, not the heart. No one is able to avoid the reality that life provides many opportunities for experiencing evil and pain firsthand. In fact, the problem of evil is considered "the most serious intellectual obstacle that stands between many people and religious faith."[1] From

---

1 Francis J. Beckwith, William Lane Craig, and J. P. Moreland, eds., *To Everyone an Answer: A Case for the Christian Worldview* (Downers Grove, IL: InterVarsity Press, 2004), 203.

life's first cry, the human experience is one of pain for both the child and mother.

In addition, death involves pain, often for the dying, and always for the people who are left behind to grieve the loss of a loved one. Perhaps more obvious and disturbing is the moment-by-moment life experience that is plagued with sickness, injury, acts of violence, and other various pains and evils that lead to an unavoidable question *why?* "If . . . we follow the course on which humanity has been led, and become Christians, we then have the 'problem' of pain."[2]

C. S. Lewis documents his experience with pain in his book *A Grief Observed.*[3] Lewis, one of the most influential Christians and philosophers in recent history, worked out this issue with clarity in his book *The Problem of Pain.*[4] However, later in his life, the death of his wife moved him to challenge his own philosophical beliefs: "Don't come talking to me about the consolations of religion or I shall suspect that you don't understand."[5]

Lewis wrote:

> I not only live each endless day in grief, but live each day thinking about living each day in grief . . .
>
> Her absence is like the sky, spread over everything.

---

2 C. S. Lewis, *The Complete C. S. Lewis Signature Classics* (San Francisco: Harper San Francisco, 2002), 379.

3 C. S. Lewis, *A Grief Observed* (San Francisco: Harper & Row, 1961).

4 C. S. Lewis, *The Problem of Pain* (New York: Macmillan Company, 1944).

5 Lewis, *The Complete C. S. Lewis Signature Classics*, 449.

But no, that is not quite accurate. There is one place where her absence comes locally home to me, and it is the place I can't avoid. I mean my own body."[6]

Blinded | Pastor James Wilson

When people are asked to describe childhood, often they respond with words such as *innocence, family,* and *peaceful.* When I think back to my childhood, those are not the first words that come to mind. When I was in third grade my entire world changed. I was only nine years old, but I was learning quickly what it meant to live in a broken home. My parents divorced, and I moved with my mom and sister to a new town, as we began life without my dad. Learning to navigate these newfound circumstances brought challenges, but they were only complicated by what I was about to face.

As I settled into a new home and a new school, I started noticing that I was having difficulty with my vision. Slowly my eyesight worsened, as I became more and more confused by what was happening. Glasses were the immediate response, but more significant issues were going on. As my vision continued to decline, my left eye began drifting over in what is known as amblyopia, or lazy eye. I spent the majority of my childhood in doctors' offices. However, none of my appointments, scans, or exams resulted in any real answers. I remember that consuming feeling of desperation and the helpless sense of loneliness.

---

6 Lewis, *The Complete C. S. Lewis Signature Classics*, 445.

Throughout elementary school I sat on the floor at the front of the class to see better what was on the board. Some days I would have to get a paper copy of that information because reading it from the board was too difficult. Middle school didn't get any more comfortable, and there were several times when I completely lost my eyesight due to misdiagnosed complications. There were many days when I could see only out of my right eye, and my self-confidence was almost nonexistent. As the impact of my condition grew, so did my insecurities, and I carried both with me throughout my school years.

One of the most challenging struggles for me was the feeling of loneliness. The sight of couples hugging or holding hands caused me to think of all the reasons no one would ever love me. How could anyone be attracted to me when I didn't even want to look in the mirror at myself? I was thankful for the eyesight that I had, but I based my self-worth on what I was missing. On the outside I put on the smile and made all the jokes, but inside I was broken. I was alone. I didn't like who I was, and I was angry with God for making me this way. I couldn't understand why God would do this to me knowing that I would go through so much pain. I prayed countless prayers for healing, but it never came.

Life has changed a lot since childhood. My fear of spending my life alone ended the day I met my wife, Alison. She saw beyond my disabilities. She fell in love with a part of me I had been hiding for many years. I also was finally diagnosed correctly. In recent years doctors have discovered that I have a rare hereditary disorder known as Wagner's Syndrome. As a result, my connective tissues are weak, and I am always at risk for a retinal detachment.

Though some of my circumstances have changed, I know how desperation and loneliness feel. Even as a believer I know the pain of struggling with your faith when it seems your God has turned a deaf ear to your cries for help. But in those moments I find Him embracing me with grace and love. Pain is real and it hurts. Pain also brings a realization that greater strength is available to us when our power is fading. I've come to understand that I can't experience the fullness of God's sustaining grace until I find myself in need of it. When I needed Him the most, His promises became more than words on a page.

Pain brings a realization that greater strength is available to us when our power is fading.

Who Is God?

Have you ever wondered what God is really like? What images come to mind when you think of God? A.W. Tozer wrote, "What comes into our minds when we think about God is the most important thing about us."[7] Perhaps this is because we tend to become like the object we worship; so it is important to know exactly who God is. An ultimate commitment to anything less than ultimate will not ultimately satisfy. Tozer was right. The most important thing

---

7 A. W. Tozer, *The Knowledge of the Holy: The Attributes of God: Their Meaning in the Christian Life* (New York: Harper, 1961), 1.

about us is what we think of God. God is like a rope that goes infinitely in both directions. You can hold it and see it, but you can't see the ends. Although we can't know everything there is to know about God, we can know God.

> The heavens declare the glory of God;
> And the firmament shows His handiwork.
> (Psalm 19:1)

> For since the creation of the world His invisible attributes are clearly seen, being understood by the things that are made, even His eternal power and Godhead, so that they are without excuse.
> (Romans 1:20)

Tension: Good God, Evil World

God has three attributes that when looked at in combination seem to be in direct contradiction with the presence of evil in the world. "The problem of evil is grounded on the fact that a number of related and essential beliefs about God appear to be incompatible with the evil we encounter in the world."[8]

- God is all-powerful and can defeat evil.
- God is all-good and opposes evil.
- God is all-knowing and foreknew evil.

The God of the Bible is described as being infinitely powerful, good, and knowledgeable. However, if God exists and has the three attributes just mentioned, "He would have both the

---

8 Beckwith, *To Everyone an Answer*, 207.

desire and the power to rid the world of evil."[9] In addition, He would know how to do so. Let's delve a little deeper into these three attributes.

Unlimited Power

God is omnipotent and has the power to do all things that are in accordance with His character and will. The word *omnipotent* literally means that God is all (omni), powerful (potent), and is unlimited in ability. Some individuals have argued that God is not all-powerful and is limited in what He can do. One such person is Rabbi Harold Kushner. In his book *When Bad Things Happen to Good People*, Kushner argues that God is not all-powerful and that is why evil is present in the world.[10]

According to Kushner, God simply does not have the power to do anything about the evil and pain in the world, even though He may want to. However, "if this is the case, are we really talking about a God at all or just a finite creature?"[11] The backdrop of Kushner's statements is his painful experience of watching his son die at a young age.

Kushner was not willing to worship a God who had the power to stop his son's suffering and pain and chose not to do so. Kushner would consider this a morally deficient God. However, this raises an additional question: What standard is he using to judge God's morality and goodness? It would seem that Kushner is using his own personal standard to evaluate God's actions and motivations.

---

9 Norman L. Geisler, *The Roots of Evil* (Grand Rapids, MI: Zondervan, 1978), 11.

10 Harold S. Kushner, *When Bad Things Happen to Good People* (New York: Avon, 1981).

11 Geisler, *The Roots of Evil*, 27.

If God must submit to Kushner's standard, or any other, then that standard is bigger than God. Any standard God submits to would have to actually be God itself. By judging God's actions, Kushner is taking on the role of God's judge and is now acting as God. Kushner suggested that if we can bring ourselves to acknowledge that there are some things God does not control, many good things become possible. He went further to ask if we are capable of forgiving God even when we have found out that He is not perfect.

If God's power is limited, then He is simply not dependable to do what He says He will do. He may not actually have adequate power for the task. In the case of evil, God would potentially be inadequate to act against it. This would explain the presence of evil in the world. However, Christianity does not hold that God is limited in power. Christians believe that God is the one and only all-powerful Being. His almighty nature would include power over evil.

Unlimited Goodness

God is also *omnibenevolent*. Christians are usually quick to point out that "God is good all the time, and all the time God is good." Omnibenevolence is one of the most frequently taught and user-friendly attributes of God in the church today. Everyone desires for God to be a good God who loves them and wants the best for them. Kushner was so passionate about affirming God's goodness that he was willing to sacrifice God's power to affirm it.

Christianity asserts that God is not only all-powerful but is also all-good. This is what the word *omni* (all) *benevolent* (good) means. However, if God is really all-good and all-powerful, why does He allow evil and pain to occur in our lives? "If the universe is so bad, or even half so bad, how on earth did human beings ever come to attribute it to the activity of a wise and good Creator?"[12]

Some have concluded that God is not really all that good and that He sometimes does things that are unloving. However, "if God is limited in love, He must also be limited in His moral nature. This leaves us with a difficult problem. If we are faced with a morally imperfect God, how would we know it?"[13] In other words, in order to judge God's goodness, a standard of goodness must be used. As stated before, if there is a higher standard of goodness, then that standard itself would be God. In many cases, that higher standard of goodness becomes the individual's own preferences and desires. This would certainly seem to be the case in the life of Rabbi Kushner. The truth from a Christian standpoint is that "whether we like it or not, God intends to give us what we need, not what we now think we want."[14]

Unlimited Knowledge

The attribute of *omniscience* affirms that God is aware of all things, potential and actual, and that there is absolutely nothing that God does not or cannot know. This is important in dealing with the problem of evil. Because God knows everything, He would have the knowledge of how to defeat evil. He

---

12 Lewis, *The Complete C. S. Lewis Signature Classics*, 374.
13 Geisler, *The Roots of Evil*, 29.
14 Lewis, *The Complete C. S. Lewis Signature Classics*, 390.

would also have known before He created the world that evil would be a part of it. An all-knowing God would also be aware of every evil act that each individual would commit before he or she even committed it.

If God has all knowledge, then why would He not proactively stop every evil act from happening? It seems unlikely that God would know how to deal with evil and choose not to, unless He lacks either the desire or power to prevent and/or remove it. However, the God of Christianity is indeed all-good and all-powerful as mentioned above. Therefore, there is an all-powerful, all-good God that also knows everything.

Since the God of Christianity possesses these three attributes, He has the power to defeat evil, the desire to defeat evil, and knows how to defeat evil. From this understanding of God and His attributes comes the problem of evil. How did evil get here? Why does God allow it? Why does He not destroy it? These questions will be answered in the next chapter.

Author's Comments

JEFF Many years ago, when I was a student at Southwestern Baptist Theological Seminary in Fort Worth, Texas, a tragedy took place at a nearby church. A gunman opened fire on an unsuspecting crowd of young people as they attended an event at the church. I remember the pastor of that church, moments after arriving on the scene, answering the coldhearted question: "Where was your God when this happened?"

As I stood in that room on the third floor of Children's Hospital of Georgia, praying that my baby would make it through surgery, that pastor's response to tragedy rang through my mind. "He was in the same place He was when His own Son died on the cross." He was still on the throne then, and He was still on the throne October 5th as my daughter was undergoing emergency brain surgery.

I have spent the better part of my life telling people, "God is sufficient for whatever you are facing," never realizing the depth of that statement. It is easy to believe that God is sufficient when what you are facing makes sense and follows some order of how we think life should be. It's not until the very core of all that we know and love is shaken to its foundation that we begin to experience the breadth of God's promises to us. The truth of God's identity is not defined by our circumstances. However, God uses our circumstances to reveal to us more of His identity.

Where Is Your God?

God never said life would be easy and no one would ever suffer. Instead, Psalm 46 describes desperate circumstances such as this: "The earth give[s] way, and the mountains fall into the heart of the sea," and "its waters roar and foam and the mountains quake with their surging." However, that entire passage of Scripture affirms that

> God is our refuge and strength,
>> an ever-present help in trouble.

> Therefore, *we will not* fear, though the earth give way
>> and the mountains fall into the heart of the sea,
> though its waters roar and foam
>> and the mountains quake with their surging.
>> (Psalm 46:1-3 NIV, italics added)

No matter our circumstances, the truth is the truth, and truth does not change. We can choose to dwell in the first part of that verse as our world crumbles all around us and concede defeat when all we can see is the catastrophe. Or we can choose to run into our Refuge and find the strength to face our circumstances. We can decide to bow to fear and allow it to overtake us. Or we can choose to rest in the God who is bigger than our fear. In these moments, we hurt. In these moments, we feel hopeless and desperate. And, in these moments, we feel God holding us.

Green Hearts is not written to speak only to Christians. If you remember, we stated in the introduction that this book is written from a Christian perspective. Our desire is to offer hope and truth that applies to everyone who has faced tragedy, pain, and loss. However, truths that we glean from God's Word become the very foundation of our triumph over tragedy. If you have a heartbeat you have known heartache, regardless of your spiritual status. Proof of this is found in scripture passages that tell us that even as believers in Christ we will mourn, but we will be comforted. We will grieve, but we will be loved. None of us is promised a life without pain and suffering; but we are promised there is comfort and strength for those who believe.

> Who shall separate us from the love of Christ? Shall tribulation, or distress, or persecution, or famine, or nakedness, or

danger, or sword? No, in all these things we are more than conquerors through him who loved us. For I am sure that neither death nor life, nor angels nor rulers, nor things present nor things to come, nor powers, nor height nor depth, nor anything else in all creation, will be able to separate us from the love of God in Christ Jesus our Lord.(Romans 8:35, 37-39 ESV)

> None of us is promised a life without pain and suffering; but we are promised there is comfort and strength for those who believe.

What Do God and Google Have in Common?

One of the most familiar search engines on the Internet today is Google. Have you ever thought about the name *Google?* The term Google is a noun that became a verb. You have most likely heard people say, "I Googled it." Used in this way, Google is a verb. But what about the sentence, "Google is one of the most popular search engines on the Internet"? Used in this way, Google is a noun. Google is both a noun and a verb.

> Then Moses said to God, "Indeed, when I come to the children of Israel and say to them, 'The God of your fathers has sent me to you,' and they say to me, 'What is His name?' what shall I say to them?" And God said to Moses, "I AM WHO I AM." And He said, "Thus you shall say to the children of Israel, 'I AM has sent me to you.'" (Exodus 3:13-14)

God's name—I AM—is also a noun and a verb. The verb tense here is imperfect and could be translated "I Am who was, who is, and who will continue to be." God is everything that He can be—He has no potential to be anything other than what He is. God is life, and we have life because He shares it with us.

The term *Google* was originally a creative spelling of *googol*, a number equal to 10 to the 100th power. Googol was coined colloquially as an unfathomable number in the 1930s and is attributed to the nine-year-old nephew of American mathematician Edward Kasner. With this in mind, it is worth noting a striking difference between God and Google. As vast and expansive as Google is, it is limited and has potential to grow in a way that God does not.

God Has No Potential

When someone says that a person has "no potential," the statement is generally not a positive one because it points to the person's inability to develop to a higher level. However, in God's case, He has no potential because He already is at the highest level possible. He is infinite, unlimited, and fully actualized. God, then, is Pure Actuality. He *is* Being. Everything else merely *has* being. God having "no potential" is actually positive because it affirms His total completeness and lack of need (and ability) for any growth or change. I AM.

Are you reaching regularly into the riches of your relationship with God? When I need to know something, I typically search Google for an answer. However, as large as Google is, it has nothing on our God. Our God is beyond the limits of the best search engines. He is an unlimited source of knowledge and wisdom, and He is always available. Further, Scripture teaches us that God actively searches us as well. Our relationship with

Him is interactive in a way that is rich in rewards and unique from all other relationships we experience.

> "I the LORD search the heart
>   and test the mind,
> to give every man according to his ways,
>   according to the fruit of his deeds."
>   (Jeremiah 17:10 ESV)

God Is

God is immutable. The word *immutable* simply means that God is unchangeable. Nothing about His nature—His character or attributes—can change. To speak of God changing His mind or changing His will is simply wrong. "God is not man, that he should lie, / or a son of man, that he should change his mind" (Numbers 23:19 ESV). Although this subject is hotly debated in contemporary theology, it was not debated in the first nineteen hundred years of church history. Think about this:

Google has nothing on our God . . . He is an unlimited source of knowledge and wisdom, and He is always available.

- God is the uncaused Causer.
- God is the unchanging Changer.
- God is the unmoving Mover.

Just to illustrate, the sun provides light twenty-four hours a day, seven days a week. All year long, all decade long, all century long, the sun just keeps on shining. However, the earth gets dark. How can there be all that light and the earth still gets dark? It's because the earth turns. The earth gets dark because it is spinning on its axis. Therefore, the side that faces the sun gets light, and the side that is facing away does not.

If there is darkness in your life, it's not because God, the Father of Lights, is turning; it's because you are turning. He is the Father of Lights, and in Him there is no shadow (James 1:17). There is no darkness in Him. Because God is faithful, He's consistent. Just like the sun, He is always shining; and in His light, there is no shifting or moving shadow. We just have to make sure we are turned toward Him.

Why Pray?

Have you ever prayed for a miracle? "This is the confidence which we have before Him, that, if we ask anything according to His will, He hears us. And if we know that He hears us in whatever we ask, we know that we have the requests which we have asked from Him" (1 John 5:14-15 NASB).

Because God is unchanging, it is easy to wonder why we should pray. Is this passage saying that we can ask God for anything and He will miraculously give it to us? This seems unlikely based on the context. In 1 John 3:22, obedience to God's commands and a willingness to serve God by doing what pleases Him are conditions for receiving. In the passage above from chapter 5, John also adds that what we ask should be in line with God's will.

To enjoy the *power* of prayer, we must understand the *purpose* of prayer. God is not a genie in a bottle. He is an all-knowing, all-powerful, all-good Being who desires to pour out His blessings on His people. Prayer is not our way of getting our will done in heaven. It is God's way of getting His will done on earth (Matthew 6:9-10).

Prayer doesn't change God, but it changes things. God is the unchanging Changer of all things. He is the unmoving Mover of all things. Consider this illustration by Dr. Tony Evans:

> If I put a million dollars in your physical bank account, you are a guaranteed millionaire. But if you don't know how to write a check, that which is guaranteed cannot be enjoyed. Too many of us who've got bank accounts full of God's blessing are forgetting to sign our checks. We forget to draw from that spiritual reservoir, or we don't understand how to draw from that spiritual reservoir to live the successful Christian life."[15]

Prayer is not our way of getting our will done in heaven. It is God's way of getting His will done on earth.

---

15 Tony Evans, *Tony Evans' Book of Illustrations: Stories, Quotes, and Anecdotes from More than 30 Years of Preaching and Public Speaking* (Chicago: Moody, 2009), 230.

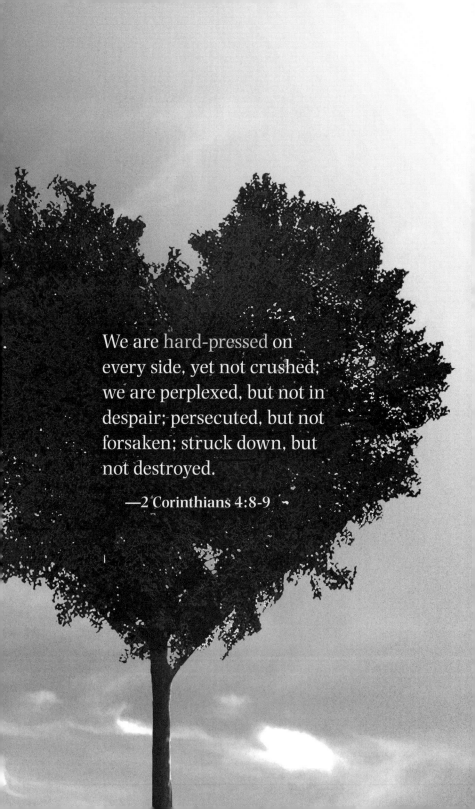

We are hard-pressed on every side, yet not crushed; we are perplexed, but not in despair; persecuted, but not forsaken; struck down, but not destroyed.

—2 Corinthians 4:8-9

CHAPTER 5

ANSWERS

Crushed | Jeff Risk

E very single one of us, at some time in life, comes to a place where something stops us in our tracks. Something dramatic happens, and we are not sure what's going on. Through an event that happened in my life, I realized that God had a particular message, and He used that experience to turn me in a specific direction.

I became a Christian at the young age of eleven years old. God helped me to see my sin, and I placed my faith in Christ. From that point sanctification began in my life. My prayer life had a richness and relevance that had not existed before. I genuinely wanted to speak with my Savior and know Him better. I quickly found myself praying all the time, speaking to God while I played Little League games and while I endured difficult situations at school. Years later, however, when I stepped out from under my family into a college setting, my choices led me down into a dark valley. I had not neglected or turned my back on the faith, but the walk.

My father was a general contractor, so I grew up in the construction industry. During the summers of my college years, I would work with him. Early one day something terrible happened. We were working on a three-story apartment complex when a full pallet of shingles and a large deck fell directly onto me. I was buried beneath five thousand pounds of rubble. I never lost consciousness, but my back and sternum were broken. I was not able to breathe. A peace that I cannot aptly describe poured over me, even as I heard my father screaming my name. He frantically removed the debris until he reached me, already finding evidence of God's hand. In the splintered rubble, a six by six post was left fully intact and was touching my body from ankle to shoulder. That post kept the sheer weight from killing me.

A few hours before that happened, the doctor who would be on call at the hospital emergency room was at home, restless. He said later that he was not a person who had insomnia; but for some reason that night, he was awake. In an attempt to prompt sleep, he picked up a trade journal and read an article about a medicine that had been around for a long time but was being used in a new way to treat spinal cord patients. This was new information for him, and after reading that article, he slept.

Only a few hours later the doctor awakened and made his way into work. Almost immediately after his arrival I was wheeled into the hospital. Because I was a spinal cord patient, he administered that medicine to me. This doctor said that his reading that article at that time "was no coincidence." We learned later that the medicine was critical to my eventual recovery.

The emergency room doctors and staff pricked my feet to determine if I had any feeling. I didn't. I couldn't move anything.

The X-rays exposed the fact that I had three broken vertebrae, the middle of which resembled a crumbled cracker. The doctors used this evidence, along with the fact that I couldn't move or feel, to declare unequivocally that I was paralyzed and would never walk again. This was devastating news to my parents and brother, but I had a strange confidence that I would be OK.

The determination was made to transport me by helicopter to a hospital that was better equipped to help me. Amazingly, the man who tended to me on the helicopter quizzed me about my background; and, after a short discussion, he and I decided to sing hymns on the ride to the new hospital.

Two days later I was wheeled into eight hours of surgery. I had two rods and nine pins inserted into my spine. Those hours were agonizing for my mother and father. When the surgery was finished, the door at the end of the long, long hall swung open, and the surgeon stepped out, weeping. The thought that I might have died during the operation went through my parents' minds. The doctor walked slowly toward them, and they rushed down the hall. He looked them in the eyes and told them that the evidence and severity of my injury did not leave room for anything but paralysis; "Yet," he said, "his spinal cord was not severed, and he will make some sort of recovery. I did not do that." We found out later that this surgeon was not a Christian; yet he gave glory to God, affirming in specific terms that a miracle had occurred.

By this time there were hundreds, if not thousands, of people praying for me. The day after my surgery, as I lay in bed, I could feel God answering prayers. The best I could describe at the time was that I could feel the prayers entering my body. It was not long before I had a feeling well up in me to walk. When the doctor made his rounds, he stepped into my room, still visibly shaken. He was told by the nurses, almost jokingly, that I wanted to get up and walk. He turned to the nurses with a very serious look and said, "Who am I to tell this boy that he can't get up? Get him up!" So my father and brother got on each side of me to help me out of bed so I could try to stand. I shuffled my feet across the floor.

I spent the next year recovering. During that time God delivered a message to me. The dark valley that I had walked down was not what He had in mind for me! God had never left me, even when my actions were not honoring to Him, and He had not left me in my darkest hour. I took the Lord's hand, and He led me out of that dark valley. I learned at a young age that what God says in Scripture has value is indeed what is valuable When you're lying flat on your back, not able to do anything for yourself, what do you have? At that moment my accomplishments didn't matter. The fact that I was a college athlete meant nothing. The schooling I had completed was worthless. Who cared what car I was driving or how much money I had? None of that matters in life; it all falls away to less than nothing. What we do have is God and the gift of those He has put around us in our lives. All we need is the Lord.

> What we have is God and the gift of those He has put around us in our lives.

Crushed but Not Destroyed

Then Moses said, "I will now turn aside and see this great sight, why the bush does not burn." So when the Lord saw that he turned aside to look, God called to him from the midst of the bush and said, "Moses, Moses!" And he said, "Here I am." Then He said, "Do not draw near this place. Take your sandals off your feet, for the place where you stand is holy ground." (Exodus 3:3-5)

After forty years of serving and learning in the courts of Pharaoh, Moses is now at the end of another forty years of his life as a shepherd. It is worth noting that Moses meets God at the same mountain where God will later give him the Mosaic law. The bush that Moses sees is on fire but is not being consumed. Fire is often symbolic of God's presence and is also present when God descends on Mount Sinai in Exodus 19:18.

The burning bush in these verses may also represent the nation of Israel. Israel had been *crushed* by bondage in Egypt, but they would not be *destroyed*. This was the first time God had revealed Himself to Moses, or anyone else in Scripture, for more than 430 years. Later in history, God broke another 400 years of silence when John the Baptist and Jesus appeared and led an even more significant exodus. Here, God called Moses to deliver a *crushed* nation before they were *destroyed*.

Answers to the Hard Questions

At least three specific problems flow directly from an understanding of God's infinite power, goodness, and knowledge. First, how and why did an all-good God create evil? Second, why does an all-powerful God allow evil to continue? Last, why would God not defeat evil if He has the power, knowledge, and the desire to do it?

The Beginning of Bad

Q. 1: Why did God create evil?

In Genesis 6 "the Lord saw that the wickedness of man was great in the earth, and that every intent of the thoughts of his heart was only evil continually" (Genesis 6:5). But how did this happen? All throughout the creation account in the beginning of Genesis, God affirmed that His creation was good. "Then God saw everything that He had made, and indeed it was very good" (Genesis 1:31).

What happened between chapters 1 and 6 of Genesis? From where did this evil come? How did God's good creation turn out to be evil? The God of the Bible is clearly described as the Creator of all things. Even angels and the heavens are created and are dependent on God for life and existence. There is nothing, other than God, that was not created by God. This is what Genesis affirms in the creation account; *God did it!* However, from this understanding of God as Creator comes a collision with Him as all-good.

How could God create something that is contrary to His nature and character? Whatever God creates has to be good because He is essentially good, and what flows from Him in the creation process must also be good. However, evil is real; and the question is, where did evil come from if it did not come from God who is the Creator of all things? The following argument is one that might indicate that God is the Creator of evil.

1. God is the author of everything.
2. Evil is something.

3.   Therefore, God is the author of evil.[1]

This argument is valid, but it is not sound. The second premise, "Evil is something," is incorrect. Evil is not a "thing." For example, darkness is really an absence of light and is therefore not a thing but rather the absence of a thing. This is similar to the relationship between evil and good in that evil relies on good for its very definition.

The analogy of light and dark is still in need of clarification, because evil is more than just the absence of good; it is the *privation* of good. Absence only implies that something is not there. Privation implies that something ought to be present and it is not. An example that would illustrate the difference between an absence and a privation would be a blind man versus a blind rock. Sight is not expected in a rock; therefore, blindness would be an absence of sight. However, for the man, sight is expected; therefore, the blindness is a privation of sight. "Evil exists in a good thing as a lack or imperfection in it, like a hole in a piece of wood."[2] To say that evil is a "thing" is not true.

The conclusion that God authored evil based on it being "something" is also not true. Everything that God created was good at the point of creation. Although God is not the Creator of evil, He is the Creator of the good creatures who choose to do evil. God created a world in which evil was possible, but it was the creatures who actualized evil by choosing things that were not good. "He created the **fact** of freedom; we perform the

---

1   Norman L. Geisler and Ronald M. Brooks, *When Skeptics Ask* (Wheaton, IL: Victor Books, 1990), 60.
2   Geisler, *The Roots of Evil*, 20.

acts of freedom. He made evil **possible**; men made evil **actual**."[3] Did God make a mistake? No, we did!

Give Me a Break

Q. 2: Why doesn't God step in and stop evil?

Now that we understand that God did not create evil, we have a second question: Why does God allow evil to continue? Because God is all-knowing, He would have known that men would choose to do evil. Specifically, He must have known that Adam and Eve would be disobedient in the garden and that evil would be the result. So why did God allow this to happen? Even if God is not the author of evil, it would seem that His omnipotence would allow Him to keep evil from happening through either a miraculous event or other preventative measures.

In God's sovereignty, He gave humanity free will.

Why could God not have blown a great wind that made it impossible for Eve to get to the fruit she was tempted to eat? It seems that God could also miraculously turn a gun into a banana just before a murder happens. Could God have stopped the events of 9/11 by causing each of the terrorists to have a spontaneous heart attack before they killed thousands of people?

How many people have prayed to God for healing when they heard the words, "You have cancer," yet they have died anyway? "We can, perhaps, conceive of a world in which God

---

3 Geisler and Brooks, *When Skeptics Ask*, 63.

corrected the results of this abuse of free will by His creatures at every moment . . . but such a world would be one in which wrong actions were impossible, and in which, therefore, freedom of the will would be void."[4]

An understanding of why God allows evil to continue begins with a proper understanding of free will and the fall of humanity. Free will is one of the "good" things that God created. "Free will means the ability to make an *unforced decision* between two or more alternatives."[5] There is nothing evil about free will, but a person can use the free will God gives him to make choices that are contrary to God's will. What if God prevented every evil act from happening? God can't stop all evil acts without destroying all freedom to choose between good and evil, which would remove free will.

In God's sovereignty, He gave humanity free will.

Knowing that His actions would lead to the fall of humanity, the death of His Son on the cross, and the suffering of many people who would spend eternity in hell, could God have just not given man free will? At first this option makes sense. However, the only way for God to allow love to be shared between a creature and a Creator is for both to choose to participate in the relationship. Love cannot be forced, because forced love is not love at all. If the potential exists for a person to choose to have a relationship with God, it would follow that the potential for humans to not choose God would also have to be real. This is why God allowed for the possibility of evil and why free will is

4 Lewis, *The Complete C. S. Lewis Signature Classics*, 382.
5 Geisler and Brooks, *When Skeptics Ask*, 63.

a good thing for Him to have created. Free will is the only way for humans to have the potential to love God.

Why does God allow evil? If He didn't, there would be no freedom to choose good. In God's sovereignty, He gave us free will. Evil exists in our world as a direct result of humanity's abuse of free will. Free will was part of God's good and perfect creation from the beginning. However, since the time of Adam and Eve, humanity has chosen to use it for selfish motivations.

Let's Get This Over With

Q. 3: Why doesn't God destroy all evil?

C. S. Lewis noted that God must be terribly offended at our behavior. He wrote, "We actually are, at present, creatures whose character must be, in some respects, a horror to God as it is, when we really see it, a horror to ourselves. This I believe to be a fact: and I notice that the holier a man is, the more fully he is aware of this fact."[6] Why does an all-good and all-powerful God not just destroy evil and remove it from the world? "The classic form of this argument has been rattling through the halls of college campuses for hundreds of years."[7]

1. If God is all-good, He would destroy evil.

2. If God is all-powerful, He could destroy evil.

3. But evil is not destroyed.

4. Hence, there is no such God.[8]

---

6 Lewis, *The Complete C. S. Lewis Signature Classics*, 396.

7 Geisler and Brooks, *When Skeptics Ask*, 63.

8 Geisler and Brooks, 63.

This argument is valid and seems to stop Christians from being able to fully deal with the problem of evil. However, it is not true, because it leaves out one crucial word: *yet*. Just because God has not yet defeated evil, this does not mean that evil will not be defeated or destroyed by God in the future. In fact, the argument seems to boomerang on itself and point to the absolute necessity of God to one day deal with evil. Instead of working against the Christian worldview, this line of thinking actually works to support it, predicting what God's response to the evil and pain in the world will be. "Since we have not yet finished with history, it is possible that all evil in history will one day cease."[9]

In fact, the only way to refute the potential for God to one day destroy evil would be to see all of time, which only an infinite being could do. One would actually have to be God to have a vantage point that could affirm or deny that evil will be dealt with sometime in the future. Even Rabbi Kushner admits that he would believe in an all-powerful God if and when he witnessed God's righteous judgment and defeat over the evils of this world.[10]

Of course, it is not a difficult task to find biblical support for both the official defeat of evil (the resurrection) and the actual defeat of evil that will occur at a future time. Christ's victory over the grave was the first part of God's work to defeat the evil in the world.

---

9 Geisler, *The Roots of Evil*, 35.

10 "Why Do Bad Things Happen to Good People? With Dr. Norman Geisler and Rabbi Harold Kushner – Program 6," Questions from the Audience-Part 2 transcript, *The John Ankerberg Show*, accessed February 5, 2019, https://www.jashow.org/articles /why-do-bad-things-happen-to-good-people-with-dr-norman-geisler-and-rabbi -harold-kushner-program-6/.

He has made alive together with Him . . . having wiped out the handwriting of requirements that was against us, which was contrary to us. And He has taken it out of the way, having nailed it to the cross. Having disarmed principalities and powers, He made a public spectacle of them, triumphing over them in it. (Colossians 2:13-15)

Inasmuch then as the children have partaken of flesh and blood, He Himself likewise shared in the same, that through death He might destroy him who had the power of death, that is, the devil, and release those who through fear of death were all their lifetime subject to bondage. (Hebrews 2:14-15)

And He Himself will rule them with a rod of iron. He Himself treads the winepress of the fierceness and wrath of Almighty God. (Revelation 19:15)

"And God will wipe away every tear from their eyes; there shall be no more death, nor sorrow, nor crying. There shall be no more pain, for the former things have passed away." (Revelation 21:4)

Because God has not yet removed evil, we live in an evil world that results in pain and suffering. The argument that was stated above should be altered to the following:

1. If God is all-good, He will defeat evil.
2. If God is all-powerful, He can defeat evil.
3. Evil is not *yet* defeated.
4. Therefore, God can and *will one day* defeat evil.[11]

---

11 Geisler and Brooks, *When Skeptics Ask*, 64-65.

The analogy of a symphony orchestra works well to illustrate this point. Imagine that the entire universe is a philharmonic orchestra in concert; we might designate certain objects as instruments. A series of events or an era in history might then represent a particular movement within the overall concert. The death of an innocent man during this era might be represented by a dissonant chord and the Second World War by several measures of the score. If the symphony had been playing for thousands of years, and someone listened to only a few minutes of the very dissonant section, he would not be fair in pronouncing the whole symphony "horrible" or the dissonant part "unjustified." In the same way, it may be that there are some examples of suffering that do not seem justified from our vantage point, but these may nevertheless be ultimately justified.[12] God *can* and *will* defeat evil one day.

God *can* and *will* defeat evil one day.

---

12 Geisler, *The Roots of Evil*, 37.

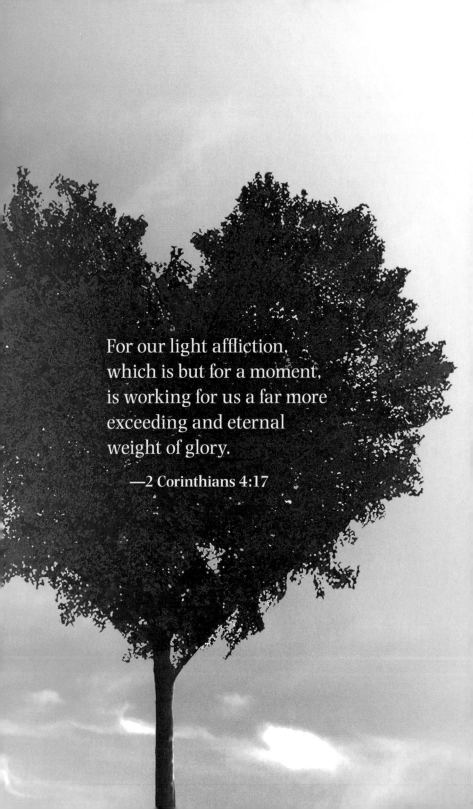

For our light affliction,
which is but for a moment,
is working for us a far more
exceeding and eternal
weight of glory.

—2 Corinthians 4:17

CHAPTER 6

SURPRISES

Joshua

On September 5, 1989, Joshua was born in a New Orleans area hospital. However, what began as a joyous time of celebration over the birth of a child quickly became a fight for life. Upon delivery, Joshua inhaled amniotic fluid, causing a microscopic hole to develop in one of his lungs. Immediate precautions had to be taken, and medicine was administered to help guard against infection.

As with any emergency, special safeguards must be in place to give the patient the best chance for recovery. This is especially true in the case of a newborn. Unfortunately, the medication levels were not monitored properly, causing toxic levels to rise in Joshua's bloodstream. At just three months old, he was placed on peritoneal dialysis as his kidney function continued to plummet.

At the age of two, Joshua received his first kidney transplant from his mother. It was a perfect match, and immediate signs of improvement were evident. The very person who had given him life had also saved him. With his restored health, Joshua was able to live a pretty happy and normal childhood. As with all organ recipients Joshua took antirejection medications daily to help his body to continue to accept the new kidney.

Although the need for antirejection medications continues for a lifetime, it was all Joshua had ever known and was a normal part of his every day. Joshua experienced many years of good health, but doctors discovered that the very medications he was taking to help his body accept the organ were now beginning to destroy it. Joshua was in desperate need of another kidney transplant.

Through the generosity of a stranger, Joshua received a living donor's kidney and soon began to live a normal life again. Unfortunately, his newfound health only lasted for three short years. Joshua contracted the Epstein–Barr virus, which would cause five years of struggles. It was yet another setback in what had been a life struggle for normalcy.

In the end, doctors discovered that the illness caused Post-transplant Lymphoproliferative Disease. PTLD occurs in less than one percent of all transplant patients. This disease was aggressive; it attack Joshua's throat, nose, tongue, and nasal cavity. Through surgeries and treatments, this cancer was removed from all areas of Joshua's body, including the removal of a lymph node located in his neck.

Joshua seemed to have fought another battle and won. However, during this process, doctors had to reduce all of the immunosuppression that Joshua had been receiving to give him the best chance to survive the disease. It was a risky move but one they felt they had to make. Unfortunately, Joshua began to reject his kidney, leading to another stint on dialysis.

Not only were these medical issues taking a toll on Joshua's body physically, but they began to impact his emotions and state of mind. The life of someone on daily dialysis can often be one filled with defeat and depression. What had been a physical challenge throughout his life was now becoming an emotional one as well. Joshua continued on dialysis for one year when "bad" suddenly became worse.

One year into his new stint with dialysis, Joshua suffered a brain bleed. He was rushed into emergency surgery to repair the bleed with no guarantee of what the outcome might be. His family had watched him win fight after fight, but this was not one they ever expected to encounter. As the surgery stretched on, Joshua's family awaited, with high anxiety, news from the surgical team.

Soon the family received the news they had hoped to hear. The surgery was a success, and the bleed was stopped. However, there was still a long road ahead. Following surgery, Joshua had lost his ability to write, walk, and speak. These essential human functions were merely out of reach for him and required extensive therapy if he was ever going to regain those abilities. Each day was a fight, but Joshua fought hard. He and his family began to see great strides as every uphill battle was conquered.

With Joshua on the road to recovery, he and his family felt stronger and motivated as every day brought another accomplishment. Joshua had always been a fighter, and now he was proving that he could not only fight but win. However, tragedy was about to strike yet again. When it appeared he had nearly fully recovered, a second brain bleed occurred, and Joshua was rushed in for another emergency surgery.

Stephanie

On August 30, 1993, Stephanie was born in a New Jersey area hospital. Early respiratory issues were soon discovered, followed by numerous tests. Through months of struggles, Stephanie was diagnosed with a lung disorder called Desquamative Interstitial Pneumonitis. What most people take for granted became a fight for every breath for Stephanie. For much of her childhood an oxygen tank became her constant companion.

As with anyone who has respiratory issues, allergens began to cause significant complications. Living in Georgia, Stephanie faced the decision to stay or move to a more conducive climate for her condition. The hopes of alleviating many of her daily struggles drove her to make a move to Miami, Florida. She soon saw improvement, and it seemed her decision was the right one. Before long, she was able to navigate most days without the aid of an oxygen tank.

What appeared to those on the outside as a lung disorder that would cause Stephanie the inconvenience of doctors' visits and oxygen tanks was causing irreparable damage to her body. As time passed, even in her new location, Stephanie continued to struggle with her breathing. Soon it became too much, and she found herself at the hospital for more testing. Through the years Stephanie's lung condition had not only caused the deterioration of both lungs, it had also done irreparable damage to her heart. She was now fighting for her life and in need of a double lung and heart transplant.

Stephanie's strength weakened. It was as though each breath she took brought her one step closer to her last one. She had fought her entire life; from infancy, Stephanie struggled for life at every opportunity. Now, surrounded by family in her Miami hospital room, Stephanie began to express to those who had fought at her side her entire life that she was tired of fighting.

Saddened by what seemed to be the end, those Stephanie loved most stood by her, even in her decision to let go. She said her goodbyes to each one as she drifted in and out of consciousness. A lifelong battle had finally taken its toll, and Stephanie was exhausted. She had done all she could do, concluding that she had nothing left to give.

Ella

On March 1, 2006, Ella was born in a Memphis area hospital. All indicators were that she was a healthy baby girl, the third child of what would later become a four-child family. Ella was outwardly shy, yet she claimed the spotlight when she was at home. She loved singing, telling jokes, and spending time with her family. Her love of family and friends was something unique, as Ella constantly created ways to bring the family together over board games, movies, and special meals. She "loved big" and always had a special hug for a friend who needed it.

Ella was a normal little girl with her whole life seemingly ahead of her when an arteriovenous malformation (AVM) ruptured in her brain. That's how life is. The things that we label normal one day can be stripped away in an instant. Over the next few days Ella's family tried to wrap their minds around this newfound reality forced upon them. They begged God for a miracle, but each test and new examination offered no hope for recovery. For anyone who has experienced fighting for the life of a loved one, you understand the emotional and physical exhaustion it causes. To catch their breath, just for a moment, Ella's parents left her bedside and stepped outside her room.

In silence, Ella's parents walked down the hallway of the pediatric intensive care unit at Children's Hospital of Georgia. Along the way, they passed by patient rooms where other children were fighting for their lives. Each step through that unit made Ella's parents more aware of the fact that they were not alone in their heartbreak. Countless families were on their knees at their children's bedside begging God for a miracle, just like their family. It was in these moments they decided that if God did not grant them the miracle for which they were praying, they wanted Ella to be that miracle for someone else.

Ella continued to be nonresponsive. Her siblings would read to her, talk to her, and even lie in the bed with her to feel her close. The waiting room stayed filled around the clock with family, friends, and church members offering their prayers and support. Her parents were unrelenting in their petitions to God for a miracle. In the end, the miracle they had been praying for never came.

Miracles

In the fall of 2016 Hurricane Matthew stormed through the Atlantic, picking up speed and power. Soon becoming a Category 5 hurricane, it threatened to destroy everything in its path. As Matthew bullied its way through Haiti, Cuba, and the Bahamas, this powerful storm was in a position to pound the southeastern United States with deadly force. As it headed toward the coastline, reports of Matthew began making their way into Ella's hospital room.

Just a few moments earlier, Ella was declared clinically deceased. Her family was coming to grips with the harsh reality that they would soon be leaving the hospital without her. Even in the midst of these agonizing moments, Ella's parents remembered their walk through the pediatric intensive care unit and the decision they had made. They chose for Ella to be somebody else's miracle as an organ donor. Waiting for recipients seemed to be taking longer than expected. Hurricane Matthew was threatening to keep medical teams from flying in to retrieve her organs. Prayers suddenly turned toward safe travel for organ recipients and surgical teams.

> The things that we label normal one day can be stripped away in an instant.

As a man in his midtwenties, Joshua had dwindled to less than one hundred pounds as a result of daily dialysis. His hopes of finding a kidney for the third time were fading, and his family had been praying for a miracle match. Suddenly the ring of a telephone brought the news that their miracle had come. Tears flowed, and a short celebration erupted. All the possibilities of what this would mean flooded their minds. However, the celebratory hugs were quickly replaced by a mad dash to make travel plans. Joshua received an arrival deadline that he would have to meet for the organ transplant. With urgency, he and his family made their way to Maryland where the surgery would take place.

While Joshua and his family were trying frantically to get to their destination, Stephanie was saying her final goodbyes. There had been very few double-lung and heart transplants ever performed, and Stephanie had given up hope on finding a match. Like a scene from a Hollywood movie, her goodbyes were interrupted as the door opened with news of a match. A new breath of hope flooded the room as preparations quickly began for the transplant to take place.

As the lives and stories of three random families intersected, we discovered that miracles are not random at all. We often question why God allows tragedy to enter our lives; but without Ella's tragedy, Joshua and Stephanie would have never received their miracle. Only God could take a man in New Orleans, a woman in Miami, and a ten-year-old girl in Augusta and bring them together in this way.

A miracle was born out of great tragedy.

Green Hearts

The sanctuary looked like a sea of green as people wearing Ella's favorite color gathered for her funeral at First Baptist North Augusta. The fourteen-hundred-seat worship center was standing room only. Ella's classmates, along with several other students from her school, Stevens Creek Elementary, sat together to pay tribute to their fallen classmate and to support each other. Her two best friends were there as well, holding hands. For most of these children, this was the first time they had come face-to-face with the reality of death. Their teachers and parents sat scattered among them, trying their best to be strong.

Children from the church, many of whom had been with Ella that Wednesday night just minutes before she collapsed, sat throughout the sanctuary with their families. The choir was filled, though barely visible to those on the main floor through the array of flowers that filled the stage. Pictures of Ella scrolled in a slideshow on the two large screens on each side of the dozens of organ pipes.

The sight was like one never seen before, pulling people from both sides of the Savannah River, the natural divide between the states of Georgia and South Carolina. Those in attendance scaled widely from retired teachers to local politicians and everyone in-between. The story of this little girl had spread far and wide, and communities from multiple counties and states were drawn to share their condolences.

The procession of family cars lined the street in front of the church as the lobby doors opened and Ella's loved ones began to file in slowly. The look of shock and disbelief still showed in their tired, tearstained eyes as someone approached and started putting green bracelets on each of them. Ella's PICU doctor had the bracelets made to read #*forella*, and she and Ella's nurses were in attendance. A silent hush fell over the room as the family made their way down the aisle to occupy the reserved seating near the stage. The service was Christ-centered as songs were sung and stories were told, but in the end, the room was filled with shattered hearts and saddened faces.

Soon after the service ended, the family was escorted out of the church and back to the cars for the ride to the cemetery. As they filled the cars, those inside the church quickly spilled out to line the streets. As the family pulled away, the impact their little girl had on that community was on display. Business owners dressed their storefronts in green ribbons and signs. Large green hearts were displayed along the road among the crowds of people holding green balloons. The balloons were released as the family cars passed. It was a scene that one might expect to see at a royal funeral.

It is extremely unusual that a ten-year-old girl could have such an impact on a community she had been a part of fewer than four years. Social media was covered in green hearts by people all around the world. Hearing the news of Ella's collapse, Christian artists Point of Grace and Jason Crabb stopped their concerts to pray for Ella. An underground church in Iraq reached out to Ella's family to share the news of a special prayer service taking place for her.

More than 76,000 viewers tuned in to see a Facebook Live video from Ella's family shortly after her passing. One can only conclude that the reason her story so significantly impacted people from every walk of life all around the world is that Ella could have been their daughter or granddaughter. She could have been their student or their child's best friend.

Reunited Hearts

Ella's death was mainstage in so many ways because her father is onstage every week. Whether in industry circles as a Dove Award-winning songwriter or in the community as the worship pastor of First Baptist North Augusta, Jeff is often in the public eye. As this horrific event unfolded, hundreds of texts and phone calls began to pour in within the hour. In the hospital the family quickly learned that they had to put their phones away to be able to process what was happening.

Life as a public figure has its challenges, but it serves as a benefit in many ways as well. This became evident during the *Ella's Acts of Kindness* drive the family holds each year on her birthday. At the request of Ella's family, people from coast-to-coast performed acts of kindness in her memory on the following March 1st. Locals who participated in the day were invited to the church for cake and to share the impact their kindness had on those who received it. Nobody could have guessed what other surprise was awaiting those in attendance.

As a surprise for Ella's mom, Jody, Jeff flew in Stephanie, Ella's heart and lung recipient, for Ella's birthday. Not only was the family able to meet her for the first time in person, but those who came to the party got to meet her as well. The following Sunday, that same moment happened onstage during the morning worship service as the people were once again dressed in green to show their support for Ella's family. Jeff sat at the piano as Stephanie and Jody were brought onstage together.

As Stephanie and Jody walked out, Jody was carrying a stuffed animal in her arms. It was a bear, a gift from Stephanie. On the outside of its chest was an embroidered green heart, but inside its chest was the recording of Ella's heartbeat, now beating inside of Stephanie. To wrap your arms around someone, knowing your daughter's heart still gives life with every beat, and her lungs still give life with every breath, is an overwhelming feeling. As these hearts were reunited, it was a fantastic moment that was made even more special by having the entire church share in it together.

When we fully trust God, we trust in the tragedy as well as in the triumph.

Jeff began to play quietly from the piano. It was a song, *With Every Heartbeat*, written by Jeff with a friend, Joel Lindsey, for this moment. The lyrics elegantly describe God's sovereignty and faithfulness to bring life from death and hope from hopelessness.

With every heartbeat
Lord You are faithful
Faithful again and again
Down here on earth
And then up in heaven
From the beginning to end
With every heartbeat
With every heartbeat
With every heartbeat Lord
You are faithful
Just like You've always been[1]

How can a father who has lost his child proclaim these words in the face of such a tragedy? They can flow only from the heart of someone who has experienced God's overwhelming love. When we fully trust God, we trust in the tragedy as well

---

1   © 2018 Sunset Gallery Music / BMI, Dayspring Music, LLC, Songs From the Inside / BMI

as in the triumph. Our hope in Him doesn't come and go with our understanding. He never promised us that faith would be easy. Instead, it's in the most challenging times in life that our faith grows strong as the *whys* outweigh the *reasons*.

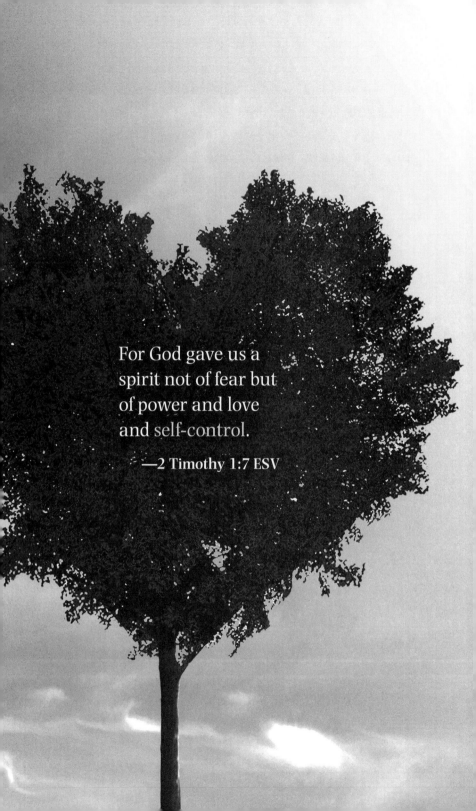

For God gave us a
spirit not of fear but
of power and love
and self-control.

—2 Timothy 1:7 ESV

CHAPTER 7

GRACE

My Sister Was Murdered | Paige McLemore

My life changed in October of 1988. I was eighteen and was beginning my freshman year of college. My older sister, Lee, was also in college and was entering her sophomore year. We did everything together, so it only made sense that we would both attend the same school. We shared a room, a car, and even shared friends. Thursday, October 26, began as a typical day. We both had part-time jobs; and, after class, Lee dropped me off before heading to her job at a local sporting goods store. If I close my eyes, I can still see her as we said goodbye for the last time.

Lee's shift started as usual but was quickly interrupted as a man entered the store. Stealing a pair of shoes and sweatpants, he began his getaway. One of my sister's coworkers shouted at the thief. She told him that she was calling the police and would identify him. Those words got his attention, and he began to reenter the store. However, instead of returning the items and leaving, he approached my sister and her coworker with a gun and shot them. "Execution style" is the way local newspapers described the senseless murder of my sister. When I got the news, my world stopped. In the days, weeks, and months that followed, our family's lives were consumed with funeral services, interviews, visiting family and friends, and a painful murder trial.

As time moved us further away from the initial loss, all of the attention surrounding Lee's passing also ended. The responsibilities of work and school marched on, but I was at a standstill. Daily activities triggered my pain again and again. Lee and I had shared several classes that year. I asked myself, "How can I go back to class and stare at her empty desk day after day?" Dropping out of school became the only option for me as the hate in my heart for this murderer consumed my every thought. I wanted my sister back; knowing that she was gone was more than I could process. I searched for ways to cope with emotions that were out of control. For years I moved from one mistake to another as I searched for love and purpose. Loneliness became a part of who I was, and I had no way of changing my new reality.

As the years passed, I carried my pain and loneliness into marriage and the birth of a child. Though I seemed happy to those around me, I was daily covering up the pain of my loss and grief. I eventually reached out to a pastor who helped me get clarity on my thoughts and questions. I also began searching through God's Word. With Scripture becoming a daily part of my routine, my questions started to become more about who I am and less about my circumstances. As I developed a better understanding of who God says I am, I also began to understand who God says He is. God used the tragic murder of my sister, and the years that followed, to lead me to Him. However, I still had the weight of hate in my heart. I knew God was changing me, but I had no idea the magnitude of work He was preparing to do in me.

Through God's love revealed to me, I realized He had forgiven me for all the hatred and the mistakes I made after Lee was murdered. I read in Romans 3:10 that "there is none righteous" and finally forgave myself. I understood what it means to be forgiven by God. Colossians 3:13 says, "Even as Christ forgave you, so you also must do." These words stuck in my spirit, and I couldn't shake the new realization God was giving me. As much as I didn't like it, I knew what this meant. I had to forgive everyone who had ever "offended" me. I had to forgive my sister's murderer.

On October 11, 2015, I decided to forgive the man who murdered my sister. I remember the exact day. Forgiveness wasn't something that happened overnight. It was a work God did in me over many years. God has been faithful to redeem my tragedy. I still get sad. I still feel lonely without Lee. I still miss her. I think about shopping trips, nieces and nephews who will never be born, and our late-night talks as sisters. God never required me to like my circumstances; He merely asked me to trust Him through them. Trusting God means following Him. As a result, I came to a decision that brought peace I could have never imagined.

I wrote a letter to Lee's murderer. I explained to him that he must serve his time for the crime he committed, but that I had forgiven him for his sin against me. My freedom was not found in writing a letter. Instead, I wrote and sent him that letter because of the freedom that found me. When I was broken and hopeless, God freed me from that bondage. As a result, I was compelled to forgive my sister's murderer. God's grace offers the freedom that transcends our feelings and builds our faith. My years of living *in* the tragedy have become a life of living in faith *through* my tragedy. I now live with a hope that holds me through my forever loss and joy that endures the future pains of life.

The Faces of Evil

What is evil? How do we know it when we see it? When does a car or a gun take the step from being a simple mechanical device to something that can be part of a murder? How do we come to understand the devastation and loss of life caused by a hurricane; and how is that different from the events that led to the death and destruction the world witnessed on 9/11? It seems clear that there is a difference between a hurricane and an act of terrorism. Although both are evil, one is a moral evil, and one is natural evil.

"Moral evil is evil brought about by human choices and actions; any other kind of evil is what we call natural evil."[1] A murder would be considered a moral evil because one person chose to kill another. However, if a person dies in a hurricane, that would be a natural evil because it did not result from the choice and action of a human.

A significant difference between these two categories is the matter of intent. If a human chooses to take action that will result in the death of another human, that person has intended

---

1 Beckwith, *To Everyone an Answer*, 208.

to do something that they ought not to do. However, when a person dies in a tornado, it was not because the storm intended to harm the individual. It is merely doing what a storm does. There is nothing inherently evil about winds going around in a circle extremely fast. Although a hurricane has the potential to cause damage to anything it encounters, it has no intent to do evil.

Regardless of intent, evil happens. John Stuart Mill wrote: "In sober truth, nearly all the things which men are hanged or imprisoned for doing to one another, are nature's everyday performances. Killing, the most criminal act recognized by human laws, Nature does once to every being that lives; and in a large proportion of cases, after protracted tortures such as only the greatest monsters whom we read of ever purposely inflicted on their living fellow-creatures."[2]

Forgiveness

Forgiveness was a part of Paige's tragedy. She was hurt by the immoral choices made by a man who decided to rob a store and murder her sister. Have you been hurt by someone? If so, who do you need to forgive today?

Tony Evans tells the following story:

A LADY was walking her dog, and the dog was trying to get away from the leash. But every time the dog pulled away, the lady would yank it, pulling the dog back, and the animal couldn't get free. The leash held it hostage, kept it bound, and unable to break away. He couldn't break the chain.

2 John Stuart Mill, *Nature, the Utility of Religion and Theism* (London: Longmans, Green, Reader, and Dyer, 1874), 28-29.

Many of us today find ourselves held hostage by a leash. The links on the chain are many. There is the link of anger, the link of bitterness, the link of resentment, and the link of revenge. But no matter how many links are in the chain, they all boil down to one thing, unforgiveness.[3]

"One another" is a phrase that is used throughout the New Testament and in numerous contexts. Ephesians 4:32 says, "Be kind to one another, tenderhearted, forgiving one another, even as God in Christ forgave you." We forgive when we let go of offenses and grievances freely and graciously. Because God has forgiven us freely in Jesus Christ we should be willing to forgive one another. Demonstrating an attitude of regular forgiveness will greatly enrich any relationship. We don't forgive people because they deserve it; we forgive people because we have been forgiven. The cross is a reminder of these words: *I forgive you.*

We don't forgive people because they deserve it; we forgive people because we have been forgiven.

Forgiveness is a choice to not bring the incident up and use it against the offending person. Jesus gave us the proper order of dealing with conflict. He said the first step is to confront the individual one-on-one. This should be done before you involve other people. Talking to other people, without speaking to the one you are discussing, quickly becomes gossip. While we are talking about the situation, oftentimes the individual has

---

3 Evans, *Tony Evans' Book of Illustrations*, 335.

no idea what he or she did wrong. Because of this, nothing constructive happens to help that person see his or her fault. How can a person grow and learn to be more like Christ if no one ever comes to him or her in a spirit of love and restoration? Second Corinthians 13:11 in the New International Version tells us to "strive for full restoration" and to "encourage one another."

Forgiveness is also an intentional choice to not allow the incident to come between you and the other person, "endeavoring to keep the unity" (Ephesians 4:3). Too often we brush issues under the rug or wait until a future time to bring them up. We are all humans with emotions; and, typically, the longer we wait, the more hurt builds. There may need to be some time to "cool down," but never let a situation start to rot. Forgive one another in the same way, to the same degree, and with the same intensity as Jesus forgives you.

There are three basic steps to forgiveness.

1. Identify the people with whom you're angry.
2. Determine what they owe you.
3. Cancel their debt.

The apostle John said, "There is no fear in love. But perfect love drives out fear, because fear has to do with punishment. The one who fears is not made perfect in love" (1 John 4:18). Never let fear slow you down. Many people do everything possible to avoid conversations that feel uncomfortable. The problem is that more damage is done when we avoid a situation and carry around frustration, hurt, and anger against a person. We quench and grieve the Spirit of God when we choose to hold things in rather than love one another.

God Knows Everything

What are you trying to hide from God?

Have you ever realized that you didn't know something important you needed to know in order to finish a task, such as taking a test or assembling a new purchase? When this happens, it can make us feel insecure about our ability to complete the task. But we can rest in the simple truth that our God knows everything.

Because God knows all things, we can be confident in Him and before Him. The big word for God's knowledge of everything is *omniscience*. Dr. Norman Geisler wrote, "God knows everything—past, present, and future; He knows the actual and the possible; only the impossible is outside the knowledge of God."[4] The writer of Hebrews said, "Nothing in all creation is hidden from God's sight. Everything is uncovered and laid bare before the eyes of him to whom we must give account" (4:13 NIV).

What is the point of trying to hide something from our God? We are often aware of failure within us that others may not see. However, God knows all things, and His desire is for each of us to find rest in Him. His grace is greater than all our sins. If we are troubled by uncertainty because of our failures, God wants us to continue to trust.

Feelings, Facts, and Faith

Warning: You will never *feel* exactly the same way God does about your pain, and the *facts* don't always satisfy because you

---

4 Dr. Norman Geisler, *Systematic Theology, Volume Two: God/Creation* (Minneapolis: Bethany House, 2003), 180.

can never get all of the information. It is only by *faith* that we move forward. Choose the faith track. As Christians, we have an amazing future ahead of us. Experiencing new life through faith in Christ is truly overwhelming, but the best is yet to come. Paul wrote about this to the church in Philippi: "For our citizenship is in heaven, from which also we eagerly wait for a Savior, the Lord Jesus Christ; who will transform the body of our humble state into conformity with the body of His glory, by the exertion of the power that He has even to subject all things to Himself" (Philippians 3:20-21).

This world is not supposed to be the best of all possible worlds. This is the best of all possible ways to the best of all possible worlds. When you go through difficult times, remember that God is at work and He never wastes a hurt. Don't mistake His silence for absence. Sometimes waiting is important, so be prepared to be still and have hope. Realize you are not alone and the journey is important. Our freedom from pain is delayed but not denied. Jesus is enough. The psalmist wrote:

> Don't mistake God's silence for absence.

> The LORD is my rock and my fortress and my deliverer;
> My God, my strength, in whom I will trust;
> My shield and the horn of my salvation, my stronghold.
> (Psalm 18:2)

Ask yourself, "What is God doing here?" Ask yourself, "Will I trust Him?"

Digging Deeper

The Bible contains a number of verses that deal specifically with how we should respond to the pain and evil that we encounter in this life. We encourage you to take the time to read these slowly. Don't be in a hurry to get through them. Instead, focus on what God wants to accomplish in you as you read His Word.

> For I consider that the sufferings of this present time are not worthy to be compared with the glory which shall be revealed in us. (Romans 8:18)

> Yea, though I walk through the valley of the shadow of death,
> I will fear no evil;
> For You are with me;
> Your rod and Your staff, they comfort me. (Psalm 23:4)

> My brethren, count it all joy when you fall into various trials, knowing that the testing of your faith produces patience. But let patience have its perfect work, that you may be perfect and complete, lacking nothing. (James 1:2-4)

> And we know that all things work together for good to those who love God, to those who are the called according to His purpose. (Romans 8:28)

> Beloved, do not think it strange concerning the fiery trial which is to try you, as though some strange thing happened to you; but rejoice to the extent that you partake of Christ's sufferings, that when His glory is revealed, you may also be glad with exceeding joy. (1 Peter 4:12-13)

> In this you greatly rejoice, though now for a little while, if need be, you have been grieved by various trials, that the

genuineness of your faith, being much more precious than gold that perishes, though it is tested by fire, may be found to praise, honor, and glory at the revelation of Jesus Christ. (1 Peter 1:6-7)

And not only that, but we also glory in tribulations, knowing that tribulation produces perseverance; and perseverance, character; and character, hope. Now hope does not disappoint, because the love of God has been poured out in our hearts by the Holy Spirit who was given to us. (Romans 5:3-5)

From reading these verses it seems clear that God not only acknowledges our pain but also wants to help in times of pain and trouble. We should not be afraid of suffering. Instead, we should rejoice because God is going to work out something good because of it. Despite the fact that He is not the cause of evil, He is active in our lives to use evil for good.

C. S. Lewis wrote that "God whispers to us in our pleasures, speaks to us in our conscience, but shouts in our pains: it is His megaphone to rouse a deaf world."[5] God never wastes a hurt. An individual's response is what determines whether that person becomes better or bitter when pain comes his or her way.

Perhaps we are allowed to suffer because God is much more concerned with our character than He is with our comfort. "But you cannot argue backward and link someone's *specific* pain to a direct act of God."[6] That being said, God is more concerned with our response to pain than He is with our understanding

---

5 Lewis, *The Complete C. S. Lewis Signature Classics*, 406.
6 Philip Yancey, *Where Is God When It Hurts?* (Grand Rapids, MI: Zondervan, 2010), 84.

of the cause of pain. This can be seen in the biblical examples of both Job and Jesus.

Case Study: Job

The book of Job is perhaps the earliest writing in the Bible. Job was one of the most faithful men of his time, and yet God allowed Satan to destroy his possessions, his family, and, eventually, his health. Although Job did not die, he was tested physically, emotionally, and spiritually.

Toward the end of the book of Job, God and Job dialogue about the suffering that Job has experienced. As one might imagine, Job asks God why He has allowed this to happen to him. Philip Yancey said, "God's reply to Job comprises one of his longest single speeches in the Bible, and because it appears at the end of the Bible's most complete treatise on suffering it merits a close-up look."[7]

God's response seems to ignore Job's question of why and instead points Job to what his proper response to the events in his life should be. Job stayed true to his faith in God and worshiped Him in the midst of a horribly painful time in his life. Job also acknowledged that God was using these events for good when he said, "But He knows the way that I take; / When He has tested me, I shall come forth as gold" (Job 23:10).

In the end, Job was given more than was taken away: "Now the LORD blessed the latter days of Job more than his beginning" (42:12). This verse serves as a picture of how God will make right all of our suffering when this life is over.

---

7 Yancey, 103-104.

Case Study: Jesus

The teachings and work of Jesus Christ also deal with the problem of evil and pain. One example of this is the unnamed man in John 9 who had been born blind. When Jesus is asked why the man has been born blind, He responds that the man's blindness glorifies God (verse 3). This passage, as in Job, points to the proper response to the pain rather than answers the question asked of Jesus. "Sometimes, as with the man born blind, the work of God is manifest through a dramatic miracle. Sometimes it is not. But in every case, suffering offers an opportunity for us to display God's work."[8]

Jesus also taught that the greatest love possible is achieved when a person suffers death. "Greater love has no one than this, than to lay down one's life for his friends" (John 15:13). The writer of Hebrews gives an account of this act of greatest love by Christ: "Looking unto Jesus, the author and finisher of our faith, who for the joy that was set before Him endured the cross, despising the shame, and has sat down at the right hand of the throne of God" (Hebrews 12:2).

Christ's work on the cross was no doubt overwhelmingly painful, as was His suffering when He took on the sinfulness of the world. Through His suffering, we are made alive: "For as in Adam all die, even so in Christ all shall be made alive" (1 Corinthians 15:22).

---

8 Yancey, 85.

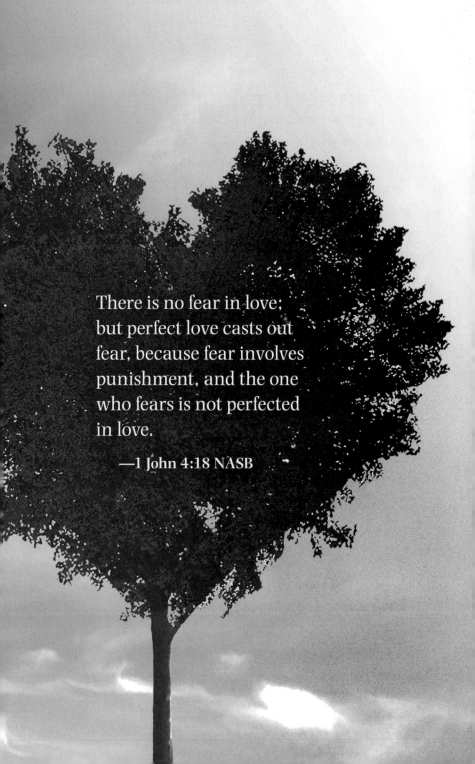

There is no fear in love;
but perfect love casts out
fear, because fear involves
punishment, and the one
who fears is not perfected
in love.

—1 John 4:18 NASB

CHAPTER 8

FAITH

Author's Comments

STEPHEN

Have you ever been in a situation that drastically changed the way you think about life? When I lived in Austin, Texas, I was invited to speak at an event for parents. As part of my talk, I decided to share a personal story about our oldest daughter Madi from years before.

I will never forget the feeling of fear that came over me on that cold December Sunday afternoon in Charlotte, North Carolina. Madi was around three years old at the time and had been feeling a little sick all morning. She was running a slight fever, but her symptoms had not been severe. In a moment, that dramatically changed. My wife ran into the room with Madi in her arms screaming.

"Help! Madi has stopped breathing!"

I took Madi into my arms and urgently told my wife, Wendy, to call 911 while I tried to figure out what was happening. Madi was still not breathing; her face was beginning to turn blue, and her eyes rolled into the back of her head. I frantically laid her down on the ground and started to give her mouth-to-mouth resuscitation with hopes of stabilizing her until help came.

Nothing I did seemed to help. She laid limp on the ground; and as time went by, I began to deal with the thought that she might die in front of me if she didn't start breathing. It was just Madi and me there on the ground, and I was as powerless as she was. Realizing there was nothing I could do, I prayed and asked God to help "my" daughter.

At that moment a thought came into my mind, and a feeling entered into my heart that has stuck with me since. "My" daughter is God's daughter first, and only He could control what happened next. I realized quickly this beautiful girl is only on loan to me. She is not mine. She has been entrusted to my care by God, who loves her, and only He is in control of her life. At that moment, I let go. I submitted and prepared for whatever the Father had for us in the moments to come. My love for God and His love for me overpowered my fear.

To make a long story short, everything in this story turned out fine. Madi made it to the emergency room and recovered sufficiently from what we found out was a significant febrile seizure. As scary as that moment was, it continues to be a powerful reminder to me as a parent that God is in control and He loves me. The love I felt from Him at that moment was powerful. It was a love that overpowered my fear and helped me to realize that fear is optional!

Once you have experienced God meeting you in a moment like that one, you see things differently. When He walks with you in the valley, it gives you a clearer vision of faith. In all of the circumstances we experience in life, God's love is intense and passionate enough to meet us before, through, and beyond our time of need.

Already ... But Not Yet

Although we are already children of God, we have not yet experienced the fullness of our salvation. Through faith, we are now God's children; but when Jesus appears we will become like Him. As we keep His promise of transformation in view and fix our desire on the goal of perfection, we will grow in purity here and now. There are three aspects to the process of our salvation.

First, *justification-salvation* is freedom from the penalty of sin and is a movement from death to life. When we believe in Jesus Christ for eternal life, we experience justification. Paul makes it clear in Ephesians 2:8-9 that justification is experienced by the grace of God through faith in Christ. Faith alone in Christ alone is the cause of our salvation from death to eternal life. It is not the *strength* of our faith but the *object* of our faith that gives us victory.

Second, once we are alive in Christ, we begin the ongoing process of sanctification. *Sanctification-salvation* is being freed from the power of sin in our lives. This ongoing transformation causes us to be more like Christ.

Last, every Christian can look forward to glorification. *Glorification-salvation* is freedom from the very presence of sin and is the ultimate state of every believer. Think about how wonderful it will be to see Jesus and to be free from all the sinful and fallen aspects of this world and our flesh.

Author's Comments

JEFF

Very few people know anything about what I am getting ready to tell you. Although, as I write this, the reality is washing over me that my previous statement will never again be true. Even so, this story is worth sharing for the point that I feel needs to be made.

I vividly remember one night, during my childhood, when one of the leaders in our church was speaking to our youth group. He was talking about faith and its purpose in our lives. I remember it well, because he made the statement that "your faith isn't for you alone." At first, I didn't agree. The very words in that statement dictate that my faith is for me. As he continued, I began to understand on a deeper level.

Faith is something we gain from experience. Even as infants, entirely dependent on someone else to provide care, nurturing, and love, we learn who the source is for those things. It is the consistent provision of those needs that reassures our faith in them. As we grow, we have blind faith that a chair is going to support our weight, based on the experiences we have from sitting in chairs. Very little examination goes into each chair we sit in before we trust it. Instead, we walk into a room, see a chair, and with blind faith we sit in it expecting it to provide comfort and support.

Let me explain on a more personal level. Most people who experience an occasional illness, such as strep throat or the stomach flu, have the symptoms and complications that come along with that. They rest and take the necessary steps to recover; soon they are better, and life is once again normal. As the dad of four children, I have come down with my share of the childhood illnesses that have invaded our home, and I have known more than my share of viruses. The difference is, when I get sick, my body shuts down entirely. I'm not talking about the pitiful drama of a man who doesn't know what to do with himself. I mean that my body *shuts down*. As far back as I can remember, this has been a recurring issue for me. If I get seriously sick, I pass out.

My wife, Jody, has laughed as she retells various times when this has happened. In our twenty-plus years of married life, she has sat with me in the rain as I lay on the asphalt beside our car in a parking lot; discovered me numerous times on the floor in the middle of the night; and come to my aid more than once as I collapsed in public. However, nothing has been quite as disturbing as the phone call she received one August morning in 2016.

My father was having outpatient surgery, and I had planned to spend time with him and my mom before the operation. I was sitting at his bedside talking with the two of them when I felt it—that awful feeling that has crept up on me so many times before. At first I felt light-headed, which soon turned into a numb feeling in my extremities. This reaction is usually followed by nausea, the sudden rising of my body temperature, sweating, and ultimately results in my being rendered unconscious.

Over the years I have learned that if I lie down and prop my feet up above my heart quickly after the symptoms begin, I have a good chance of fighting it off. The problem on this day was that I was in my dad's hospital room, and I did not want to worry him right before the surgery.

My first thought was to get out of the room as quickly as possible and find a place to lie down. That thought turned into action, as I pretended to take a phone call and made my way around my father's hospital bed and out the door. Up the hallway I went, looking for the nearest waiting room. I remember asking a nurse where that was, but I was fading fast. As she was responding to my question, I had already begun seeing stars and was trying desperately to hold on. But it was too late.

Out of the darkness, the first thing I remember hearing was a voice saying "I can't find a pulse." I knew they were talking about me, but I also knew I had to have a pulse. How else could I have heard them saying they couldn't find it? As they were trying to figure out what was wrong with me, I began to regain consciousness. I got to the point that I could understand what they were saying and respond but was so fatigued that I couldn't open my eyes. I was taken to the emergency room for testing and observation, and they contacted Jody by phone. Once again she came rushing to my side. Doctors were not able to determine what had happened, and all test results were inconclusive. As a result, they referred me to a cardiologist for more testing.

Everything, including an echocardiogram, came back normal. But there was one more test they wanted to do. So they scheduled a tilt-table test for the following week. When I arrived, they took me to the room to perform the test. I still didn't understand what was going to take place. As the doctor explained the procedure to me, it all seemed very simple and noneventful. I even remember thinking to myself, "This is a waste of time." But I did as they asked and soon found myself strapped to a table and staring at the ceiling.

Just as the doctor had explained, the table began to rise slowly, eventually placing me in a standing position. A small platform at my feet supported my weight, and I just stood there, unable to move as the doctor and nurses looked on. Seconds felt like minutes, and minutes felt like hours. As time passed, the doctor would ask if I was feeling anything. I thought, "Yeah, I feel ridiculous," but instead I answered with a polite "No, sir." At least that was my response until we entered the thirty-third minute.

Throughout the entire test, the nurses and doctor were monitoring my vitals on the EKG. Suddenly I felt that familiar feeling invading the room. I knew from the look on the doctor's face that he could tell something had changed. He stood up from his chair and asked what I was feeling. As I began to describe my symptoms, he moved closer to the EKG monitor. Sweat started to bead up all over my body as I felt myself on the edge of passing out. I could hear the beeps tracking my heart rate begin to slow as I drifted into unconsciousness.

As I awoke I didn't understand that I was waking up. It did not seem to me as though any time had elapsed. I thought I merely had my eyes closed. But I could hear the relief in the nurses' voices when I asked, "Did I pass out?"

"Did you pass out?" one nurse responded with a sarcastic laugh. "You didn't just pass out, you—well, I'll let the doctor explain."

As the doctor approached, he asked how I felt. Once he was confident I could comprehend an explanation of the test, he began to walk me through everything that happened. What we learned was, when I pass out, I am not just losing consciousness; my heart is stopping. I had entered asystole, which is the most severe form of cardiac arrest. That is why they could not find my pulse when I passed out at the hospital. I didn't have one!

During the test I flatlined the EKG for twenty-three seconds. All other tests had indicated there was nothing physically wrong with my heart. However, when my body was put through specific conditions, my heart ceased to function in the way it was created to operate. From all appearances I was physically healthy, but my body's response to stress and outside stimuli was to shut completely down. I have been given specific exercises to use when I sense these episodes coming on. They have helped tremendously, but I will deal with these reoccurrences for the rest of my life.

You may be wondering what this story has to do with the subject of this book. The answer is, this event happened two months before losing Ella, and I have experienced many similarities in my grief to my feelings during that test. Grief can often feel the way I did on that table. Time stops, and we lose all sense of reality. For twenty-three seconds my healthy heart sat still in my chest in response to the trauma happening within my body.

When we lost Ella my heart broke into pieces. I could not make sense of the world around me. For months I struggled in every moment of every day to understand how to act the way I used to act, how to think the way I used to think, and how to respond to the people around me. Grief makes you feel like a different person from the only "you" that you knew before the tragedy. After the tragedy occurs, your physical body may look the same, but you struggle to rediscover yourself beyond what has happened to you.

Grief impacts a person like a heart that stops beating.

I could have never learned this lesson before our tragedy. In all honesty, it is a lesson I wish I had never learned. I would have preferred to stay ignorant to the full weight of such debilitating suffering. Having said that, I am reminded again of the chair that our youth leader used as an example of faith. When I walk into a room, tired from the day, I can choose to sit in a chair to rest, or refuse to sit, dependent upon my own strength to sustain me. I base my decision on my faith in that chair. My experience tells me that the chair will support me, and I will find rest when I trust it to do what it is fully capable of doing. In the same way, I have a choice in the midst of my tragedy. I can turn away from God or I can choose to collapse into His arms, trusting that He is fully capable of sustaining me based on my experiences with Him before tragedy. Faith is not determined by our circumstances but revealed in the midst of them.

When tragedy comes, we lose control of our circumstances; but we do not lose our response to those circumstances. We can find our refuge and hope in God or we can choose to continue standing in the corner, refusing to trust the chair that has faithfully held us through so many weary days. Our hearts will never feel the same again. There may be a pain with every beat for the rest of our lives.

Faith is not determined by our circumstances but revealed in the midst of them.

But there's also life in every beat. Our faith in the God who sustains us when our heart races with wonder is the same God who holds us when our hearts are utterly broken. As long as they continue to beat, every broken heart has a story to tell.

> As long as they continue to beat, every broken heart has a story to tell.

From Our Hearts to Yours

So, what is your story? Life is not skipping from mountain peak to mountain peak. There are valleys. Perhaps your valley doesn't seem as deep as the ones you've read about in this book, but it's yours. Whatever your journey, never discount it. It has made you who you are. But, even more importantly, your journey is making you who you will be one day. As with any experience, whatever you've been through, and whatever is yet for you to face, it takes time to process. But, as you do, there is much to be discovered, resulting in a story that will encourage others in their journey.

If your story filled another chapter in this book, how would it end? Where is God in the midst of your circumstances? Do you trust Him with your triumphs and tragedies? This may be the closing chapter of *Green Hearts*, but your story is still being written. If you have faced a tragedy that has so altered who you are and how you respond to the world around you, start where you are, not where you wish you were. Find a professional who can help direct the next steps you need to take. As he or she helps you evaluate what has happened, and the impact the situation has had on your life, you will begin to recognize who you are becoming and who God has in store for you to be.

If you have yet to face a tragedy that has left you broken and hopeless, the chances are that one lies ahead. When that moment comes, recall what you have read from these pages and look for what God has for you in your valley. For it's in the valleys that the truth of our stories are discovered and refined. When we set out to write *Green Hearts*, we did not want to write a book that was merely full of stories. Instead, we wanted to be intentional about showing who God says He is and who God has revealed Himself to be. This book is a mess, because life is messy, and we are broken people who are walking through shattered lives. However, when we lift our eyes, we will find the goodness of God in the worst of times.

In His grace,

Jeff Bumgardner

Stephen Cutchins
Easter, 2019

About the Authors

Jeff Bumgardner is the worship pastor of First Baptist Church in North Augusta, South Carolina. He is a sought-after clinician and multiple Dove Award-winning songwriter. Holding a BA in Music from Brewton-Parker College and a Masters of Ministry from Southwestern Seminary, hundreds of Jeff's songs have been recorded, with several other projects currently in development. Following the sudden loss of his daughter, Jeff and his family developed a nonprofit in Ella's name to help those in need through acts of kindness all across the United States.

Dr. Stephen Cutchins is the senior pastor of First Baptist Church in North Augusta, South Carolina. Stephen is an author, educator, and speaker and teaches at Fruitland Baptist Bible College. He holds a Doctorate of Ministry degree from Southern Evangelical Seminary in Charlotte, North Carolina and is completing a PhD at Dallas Baptist University. Stephen is a Christian leader who helps curious and growing people answer hard questions about life, leadership, and learning, so they can know who they are and defend what they believe.

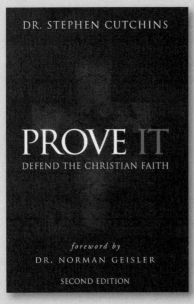

DR. STEPHEN CUTCHINS

PROVE IT
DEFEND THE CHRISTIAN FAITH

foreword by
DR. NORMAN GEISLER

SECOND EDITION

Prove it. This is the cry of a generation that is both skeptical of truth and hostile toward Christianity. Too many people are turning away from Christianity, and God, because they have questions and challenges that go unanswered. Unless the church is equipped to deal with the intellectual mind that rejects the existence of God, the objective nature of truth, and the validity of miracles, a generation will be lost to the lies and confusion of false teaching.

Prove It introduces the basic concepts, contenders, and criticisms of Christianity and prepares the reader to provide a defense for the hope that is in them (1 Pet. 3:15). Foreword by Dr. Norman Geisler.

Auxano
PRESS

For teaching guides and additional small group study materials, or to learn about other Auxano Press titles, visit Auxanopress.com.

Auxano Press Non-Disposable Curriculum

- Designed for use in any small group
- Affordable, biblically based, and life oriented
- Choose your own material and stop and start times
- Study the Bible and build a Christian library

Auxano
PRESS

For teaching guides and additional small group study materials, or to learn about other Auxano Press titles, visit Auxanopress.com.